Effective Reading

Reading skills for advanced students

Simon Greenall and Michael Swan

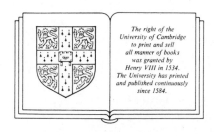

The right of the
University of Cambridge
to print and sell
all manner of books
was granted by
Henry VIII in 1534.
The University has printed
and published continuously
since 1584.

Cambridge University Press
Cambridge
London   New York   New Rochelle
Melbourne   Sydney

Published by the Press Syndicate of the University of Cambridge
The Pitt Building, Trumpington Street, Cambridge CB2 1RP
32 East 57th Street, New York, NY 10022, USA
10 Stamford Road, Oakleigh, Melbourne 3166, Australia

© Cambridge University Press 1986

First published 1986

Printed in Great Britain
at The Bath Press, Avon

ISBN 0 521 31759 2 Student's Book
ISBN 0 521 31760 6 Teacher's Book

Effective Reading

Contents

Contents

Thanks

We should like to acknowledge the help that Françoise Grellet's book *Developing Reading Skills* (Cambridge University Press), Catherine Walter's book *Authentic Reading* (Cambridge University Press) and Christine Nuttall's book *Teaching Reading Skills in a Foreign Language* (Heinemann Educational Books) gave us in preparing *Effective Reading*.

We are very grateful to the staff at the following schools and institutes who used the pilot edition and made so many useful comments: Braun AG in West Germany; the British Institutes in Paris and Rome; the British School in Florence; College of Arts and Technology in Newcastle upon Tyne; Exeter College; Godmer House School of English in Oxford; Hampstead Garden Suburb Institute in London; Inlingua in Hove; International House in Arezzo, Italy; Migros Klubschule in St Gallen, Switzerland; Stanton School of English in Tokyo; the University of Berne in Switzerland.

We would also like to thank Ruth Gairns for her comments and ideas.

Finally special thanks are due to our editors Christine Cairns, Jeanne McCarten and Margherita Baker.

Effective Reading

Notes to the user

Introduction

The aim of this book is to help learners of English to read more effectively by presenting and developing the various skills needed for successful reading comprehension. The passages are all examples of contemporary British and American English taken from a variety of sources such as newspapers, magazines, novels, advertising material and instructions. None of them have been written specially for foreign students, and only three have been adapted to make them slightly easier to understand. The book is suitable for all advanced learners of English and in particular, for students who are preparing the Cambridge Certificate of Proficiency examination. Each unit also includes a variety of suggestions for further language activities such as group discussion work, roleplays, intensive vocabulary study and writing practice. These extra activities allow the book to be used either as the basis or as part of any advanced course of English.

Structure of the book

There are 45 units in this book. Each unit contains:

- One or two reading passages
- Four or five exercises, each one designed to present or develop a specific reading skill or an examination skill (such as *Writing Summaries*)
- Suggestions for further work on the theme which has been introduced by the passage; these can be used in class or as tasks for homework.

If you choose to do all the exercises in each unit, they will take about 60–90 minutes to complete. However, it may not always be necessary to do all the exercises (see *How to use this book*). Your teacher will help you decide which reading skills you need to develop and which exercises to do.

How to read effectively

Everyone reads with some kind of purpose in mind; generally speaking, the purpose is either to enjoy oneself or to obtain information of some kind. Effective reading means being able to read accurately and efficiently, and to understand as much of the passage as you need in order to achieve your purpose. It may also be necessary to reproduce the content of the passage in some way or other, such as discussing its main ideas or writing a summary. Not everyone can read effectively even in their own language. Sometimes comprehension failure happens and the reader is unable to achieve his/her purpose. This comprehension failure may be a simple matter of not knowing the meaning of a word; but it's just as likely to be a deficiency in one or more of a number of specific reading skills. The exercises in this book are grouped under headings which refer to the following specific skills.

Extracting main ideas

Sometimes it's difficult to see what the main ideas of a passage are, or to distinguish between important and unimportant information. The exercises in this section encourage you to read for the general sense rather than for the meaning of every word.

Reading for specific information

It's not always necessary to read the whole passage especially if you are looking for information which is needed to perform a specific task. The activities here are set to practise this skill in a variety of different ways.

Understanding text organisation

Readers may sometimes have trouble in seeing how a passage is organised. The exercises in this section give practice in recognising how sentences are joined together to make paragraphs, how paragraphs form the passage, and how this organisation is signalled.

Predicting

Before reading a passage, we usually subconsciously ask ourselves what we know about the subject matter. This makes it easier to see what information is new to you and what information you already know about as you read the passage. Developing this technique ensures that as you read, you are not overloaded with too much new information.

Checking comprehension

On certain occasions, such as in examinations, you need to study the passage very closely to find the answer to a question. The information you require is in the passage; all you have to do is find it.

Inferring

A writer may decide to suggest something indirectly rather than state it directly. The reader has to infer this information, which may well be one of the passage's main points. Some readers may need practice in understanding what a sentence implies.

Dealing with unfamiliar words

One of the commonest problems facing the foreign learner is simply not being able to understand a word or expression. But it is often possible to guess its general sense by looking for clues in the context. Exercises in this section develop the skills needed to make reasoned guesses about the meaning of new vocabulary.

Linking ideas

In any passage an idea may be expressed in a number of different words or expressions. The exercises here give readers practice in seeing how different words are related to the same idea.

Understanding complex sentences

Some writers use a deliberately complicated style in which it may be difficult to distinguish, for example, main clauses from subordinate clauses. Other writers are unintentionally obscure. The effect is that it is easy to lose sight of the general sense. In this section, the reader is given practice in seeing how long and complicated sentences can be simplified.

Understanding writer's style

An important part of the pleasure in reading is being able to appreciate why a writer chooses a certain word or expression and how he/she uses it. A number of stylistic devices and features are discussed in this section.

Evaluating the text

A lot of information about the passage may be contained in the reason why it was written, or the purpose that certain sentences serve. For example, it may be important to distinguish between a statement of fact and an expression of the writer's opinion. This section helps develop the reader's more critical faculties.

Reacting to the text

Sometimes a passage may be interpreted according to the reader's own views on the subject being dealt with. In this section, practice is given in separating what the writer says from what the reader thinks.

Writing summaries

This section gives practice in what is strictly speaking a productive skill. But to be able to write accurate summaries requires accurate comprehension of the passage. Please note that the length of the summary depends on the extent of the original passage. In an examination (for example the Cambridge Certificate of Proficiency) the length of the summary varies, but it is usually up to 100 words. You may want to give your students exam practice by asking them to write shorter summaries.

How to use this book

Different learners have different problems, and as we have shown, there may be a number of reasons why someone does not read as effectively as he/she might. When you begin using this book, it may be a good idea to do all the exercises in the unit. (In particular, there are some important techniques which are presented in units 1–6 for *Dealing with unfamiliar words*; in later units, not all the difficult vocabulary is explained and you will need to use these techniques regularly.) But it's likely that you will find some exercises easier than others; in this case, you may decide that there is no point in spending too much time on these skills in later units. You should therefore concentrate on the exercises which you find more difficult in order to develop those reading skills which you lack.

If you are in a class with a large number of students, it may be difficult for your teacher to organise the correction of your work if you are all doing different exercises. However, if you work with students who need to practise similar skills to you, you can help correct each other's work.

Working with another student or in a group is an important feature of this book. It will allow you to practise your speaking and listening skills as well; indeed, some of the questions are deliberately ambiguous so as to encourage genuine discussion between you. But this will not detract from the value of the exercises if you are working on your own.

You will need to use a dictionary on occasions. If you don't have one, ask your teacher or bookseller which one he/she recommends. However, do try *not* to look up every word you don't understand. This may be difficult at first, but will get easier the more you practise the techniques in *Dealing with unfamiliar words*.

You will see from the contents page that the passages are grouped according to their general theme. This is to help you organise your vocabulary learning. But if you don't have much time on your course, it may only be possible to do one or two of the three units within each topic area (see *Contents*).

Note to the teacher or the student working alone

The Teacher's Book contains the answer key to the exercises, as well as a more complete explanation of the different skills practised in the book, and some suggestions on how to integrate the material into an advanced level course.

Unit 1   Doodles

Extracting main ideas

1 Work in groups of two or three. Look at the title of the passage below. Do you know what 'doodles' are? Ask the other students if they know.
2 Find the sentence in the introduction which explains what 'doodles' means. Did you choose the correct definition in 1?
3 The pictures are not next to the paragraphs which explain them. Read the passage through and match the paragraphs to their corresponding pictures.

Forget psychiatrists – analyse yourself with the help of doodles

Most doodles are done unconsciously when you are holding a pen in your hand and just happen to start scribbling. However, there is more to these "diagrams of the unconscious" than meets the eye. Free from the restriction of the conscious mind, they can be a useful insight into your character and personality, revealing many important aspects of your secret hopes, ambitions, fears and dreams.

1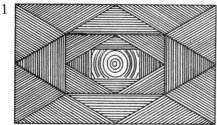

A Faces are a sign of sociability or lack of it. If you doodle happy, smiling faces (1), you have a friendly, out-going disposition which people respond to, and you enjoy an active social life. You also have a tendency to be sentimental. If your faces are grumpy (2), this may indicate anti-social tendencies. Faces looking to the right (3), are a sign of gregariousness and anticipation about the future; to the left (4), a sign of shyness and reserve.

2

B Bare or narrow trees show a lack of warmth, while landscapes demonstrate coldness and spiritual weariness. You've probably been disappointed in love or could even be suffering from a minor ailment that needs attention.

3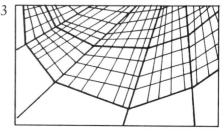

C Confused lines and squiggles show that you're a bit of a muddlehead, lacking the organisational ability to cope with everyday living. This makes for chaos and a lack of self-control.

6

4

D Houses are wish-fulfilment doodles indicating a desire for a home, family, children and happiness. How you doodle your house is important. If you have curtains at the window, smoke coming out of the chimney, little trees, flowers, figures, a path or a fence, you are seeking emotional security and a happy, fulfilled marriage away from the outside world. Beware of becoming too complacent. If your house is stark and bare with no embellishments or signs of life, no door or garden, you're lacking love and warmth in your life.

If you build a house in layers, each layer separate — you could be too houseproud, too eager to make your loved ones do your bidding and jump to attention. A little untidiness in a house makes the occupants feel comfortable, secure and happy. Are you repressing your emotions and neglecting to let yourself go now and then?

5

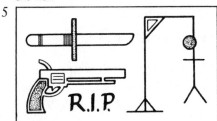

E Filled in or shaded doodles with heavy pressure are often a sign of aggression or anger. The heavier the pressure the more angry you feel; the lighter the pressure the more likely you will be to use sarcasm and a highly-developed critical faculty as a defensive measure.

6

F If your doodle resembles a web, you are making a cry for help in solving a problem. You feel trapped, and are seeking a way out; perhaps you even want to travel, try out new ideas and spread your wings. But you lack confidence to step out into the world on your own because of the web you've created around you.

7

G Knives, daggers, guns, or thin and angular strokes show aggressive behaviour patterns and sometimes even sadistic tendencies. Such things as whips and instruments of torture can reveal inherent masochistic tendencies.

8

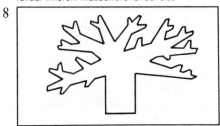

H Heavy lined shapes are often a sign that you've built a barrier between yourself and the external world. You keep your emotions in tight check because you feel that you can't cope with them and yet underneath that carefully erected barrier you know that once you meet the right person all will be well.

9

I Hearts, flowers, animals with furry coats, entwined letters and groups of faces indicate that you're in love. You enjoy day-dreaming, and building castles in the air. Sentimental, kind, affectionate and spontaneous in your emotions, you long to belong to someone special.

(Patricia Marne in *Company*)

Reading for specific information

Look quickly through the interpretations again and decide which doodles would indicate someone who is:

a) affectionate.   b) cruel.   c) disorganised.   d) happy.

Dealing with unfamiliar words

There may be some vocabulary in the passage which you don't understand. Here are two techniques you can use to guess the general sense of an unfamiliar word.

1 *Decide what part of speech the word is.*
   Look at the following words and decide whether they are nouns, verbs or adjectives.

   'angular' (paragraph C)   'embellishments' (paragraph F)
   'inherent' (paragraph C)   'repressing' (paragraph F)
   'ailment' (paragraph D)   'muddlehead' (paragraph J)
   'gregariousness' (paragraph E)

2 *Look in the context for clues to its general sense.*
   Choose the most likely answer to the following questions.

   a) 'angular': Look at the drawing. It probably has something to do with (i) shape, (ii) size, (iii) material.
   b) 'inherent': Are the masochistic tendencies characteristic of (i) whips, instruments of torture etc., or (ii) people and their behaviour?
   c) 'ailment': This is probably something which makes you feel (i) unhappy, (ii) well, (iii) ill.
   d) 'gregariousness': Faces looking to the right probably mean the opposite of faces looking to the left. So it probably means something like (i) being careful, (ii) being sociable, (iii) being pessimistic.
   e) 'embellishments': A house with no embellishments is one that is stark and bare. So it probably refers to the house's (i) shape, (ii) decoration, (iii) position.
   f) 'repressing': If you repress your emotions, you neglect to let yourself go. It means something like (i) controlling, (ii) releasing.
   g) 'muddlehead': Someone who is a muddlehead probably (i) is chaotic, (ii) copes with everyday living.

   You can check your guesses by looking the words up in a dictionary.

3 If there are any other words which you don't understand, write them down and then use the two techniques to try and guess their general sense. You may look up five of them in your dictionary. Make sure you choose them carefully.

Writing summaries

1 Read the passage again carefully, and fill in the chart below with a few of the
   words or phrases which describe the general characteristics of each type of
   doodle. In certain cases, you may have to summarise the interpretations.

webs	
knives, daggers, guns	
trees and landscapes	
faces	
houses	
filled in or shaded doodles	
hearts, flowers, animals	
heavily lined shapes	
confused lines and squiggles	

2 Decide which of your words and phrases describe positive qualities in this context
   and mark them with a + sign. Then mark the negative qualities with a − sign.

3 Look at the doodle below. Working in groups of two or three, decide which of
   the doodles illustrated it most resembles. Use the interpretation to analyse the
   person who drew it.

   Write two or three sentences, beginning like this:
   'The doodle shows flower shapes which suggest that the person is
   sentimental and kind. However. . .'

Further work

Do you know of any other ways of analysing the personality? Think about
astrology, graphology (handwriting), palm reading. Choose one and prepare a
short description of how it analyses the personality. Try and include at least ten
words and expressions from the passage.
   When you are ready, present your description to the others in the class.

Unit 2   Money is the only home

Extracting main ideas

Read the passage through. In your opinion, which of the statements below best sums up its main idea?

a) Creighton Montgomery was particularly protective of his daughter.
b) Very rich girls are rather Victorian and old-fashioned.
c) The rich still have families because of the influence of their money.
d) The generation gap only occurs in the lower and middle classes.
e) The rich can control their children's lives without being near them.
f) Marianne Montgomery lived a very sheltered life.

Marianne Hardwick was timid and unadventurous, her vitality consumed by physical activity and longing, her intelligence by indecisiveness, but this had less to do with the innate characteristics of the *weaker sex* (as her father, Creighton Montgomery, called it) than with the enfeebling 5 circumstances of her upbringing. Creighton Montgomery had enough money to mould his daughters according to his misconceptions: girls were not meant to fend for themselves, so he protected them from life. Which is to say that Marianne Montgomery grew up without making 10 any vital choices for herself. Prevented from acquiring the habits of freedom and strength of character which grow from decision-making, very rich girls, whose parents have the means to protect them in such a crippling fashion, are the last representatives of Victorian womanhood. Though 15 they may have the boldest manners and most up-to-date ideas, they share their great-grandmothers' humble dependence.
Most parents these days have to rely on their force of personality and whatever love and respect they can 20 inspire to exert any influence over their children at all, but there is still an awful lot of parental authority that big money can buy. Multi-millionaires have more of everything than ordinary mortals, including more parent power, and their sons and daughters have about as much opportunity 25

10

to develop according to their own inclinations as they would have had in the age of absolute monarchy.

The rich still have families.

The great divide between the generations, which is so much taken for granted that no one remarks on it any 30 longer, is the plight of the lower and middle classes, whose children begin to drift away as soon as they are old enough to go to school. The parents cannot control the school, and have even less say as to what company and ideas the child will be exposed to; nor can they isolate him 35 from the public mood, the spirit of the age. It is an often-heard complaint of the middle-class mother, for instance, that she must let her children watch television for hours on end every day if she is to steal any time for herself. The rich have no such problems; they can keep their offspring 40 busy from morning to night without being near them for a minute more than they choose to be, and can exercise almost total control over their environment. As for schooling, they can hand-pick tutors with *sound views* to come to the children, who may never leave the grounds 45 their parents own, in town, in the country, by the sea, unless for an exceptionally secure boarding school or a well-chaperoned trip abroad. It would have been easier for little Marianne Montgomery to go to Cairo than to the nearest newsstand.   50

(Stephen Vizinczey: *An Innocent Millionaire**)

* *An Innocent Millionaire* by Stephen Vizinczey is published in the United Kingdom by Hamish Hamilton and in the United States by Atlantic Monthly Press.

Dealing with unfamiliar words

1 Read the passage again and choose seven or eight words which you don't understand. Then use the two techniques explained in unit 1 to help you guess their general sense.

Decide what part of speech the word is.

Look in the context for clues to its general sense.

Write down what you think the word means.

2 Work in pairs. Ask your partner if he/she has written down any of the words that you have on your list. Do you both agree on their meanings? Discuss the meanings of any words which only appear on one list.   ⟫⟶

3 Each adjective in the column on the right means more or less the same as one of
  the adjectives on the left, which are taken from the first paragraph of the passage.
  Match the words with their probable meanings. Be careful! There are a few extra
  meanings on the right.

  a) 'innate' (line 4)   i)   early
  b) 'enfeebling' (line 5)   ii)   essential
  c) 'vital' (line 11)   iii) harmful and restricting
  d) 'crippling' (line 14)   iv)   modern
  e) 'humble' (line 18)   v)   lively
                                vi)   inborn
                                vii) with a low opinion of oneself
                                viii) weakening

Understanding text organisation

1 Look at these sentences and write down the main verb in each.
  a) 'Prevented from acquiring the habits of freedom and the strength of character
     which grow from decision-making, very rich girls, whose parents have the
     means to protect them in such a crippling fashion, are the last representatives
     of Victorian womanhood.'
  b) 'The great divide between the generations, which is so much taken for
     granted that no one remarks on it any longer, is the plight of the lower and
     middle classes, whose children begin to drift away as soon as they are old
     enough to go to school.'

2 Lines 1–6 express two contrasting sides of an argument in one sentence.
       'Marianne Hardwick was timid . . . by indecisiveness, *but* this had less. . .'
  Look for a second sentence in the first paragraph which contains a contrast.
  Re-write the sentence using *but*.

3 Lines 8–9 express a cause and effect.
       '. . .girls were not meant to fend for themselves, so he protected them from
       life.'
  Re-write this sentence using *because*.

4 Look for a second sentence in paragraph one which expresses cause and effect.
  Re-write it using *because*.

Understanding writer's style

In the passage, *weaker sex* is in italics to suggest that these are the words of
Creighton Montgomery, and not of the author himself. This gives the style of the
sentence an ironic effect, in which the author writes one thing but implies
something different. Look at the following extracts in their context and decide
what the writer implies by the words and expressions in italics.

a) '. . .girls *were not meant* to fend for themselves. . .' (lines 8–9)
b) '. . .whose parents have the means *to protect them*. . .' (line 14)
c) 'Multi-millionaires have more of everything *than ordinary mortals*. . .'
     (lines 23–4)
d) '. . .they can handpick tutors *with sound views*. . .' (line 44)

Further work

1 Work in groups of two or three. Using words and expressions from the passage,
   discuss and then note down what you think the author might say about rich
   people's sons. Compare your notes with a neighbouring group.

2 Now think about how you might define the *family* in the twentieth century.
   Write down a short definition and show it to a neighbouring group. Do they
   agree with you?

Unit 3   Shielding Brooke

Understanding text organisation

The following passage is taken from an article about the American film actress, Brooke Shields. There are a number of sentences missing from the passage. Read it through and decide where the following sentences should go.

a) A serious student or a movie star?

b) She is also introspective.

c) Or will she stay inside the image her mother has created for her and remain a sexy model, a pretty face which will fade in time?

d) And that famous face!

e) The marriage only lasted a few weeks after Brooke was born.

f) She looks like a housewife.

g) Now they have succeeded beyond their wildest dreams.

h) Brooke's height and looks come from her father's side.

Extracting main ideas

Choose a suitable heading for each paragraph from the list below.

a) Mother's roots.
b) Behind the facade.
c) Mothering Brooke.
d) What next for Brooke?
e) First impressions.

f) Brooke on acting.
g) A split personality?
h) Daddy's girl.
i) The family business.

1 She's a tall girl, almost gangling (5ft 11ins). She walks into the room, looking straight ahead and sits down gracefully on a 5 French chair and smiles. At eighteen, she already has a presence. (1)............... A complexion like honey and cream, green eyes skilfully made up, 10 that gaze at you bright and clear, the dark eyebrows accentuating her bone structure.

Her mother, Teri Shields, 49, hovers nearby, as always, 15 gleaming with pride. She stage-manages the interview, interrupting when she thinks it's necessary. At five feet four inches, she is cheerfully large, 20 big-breasted, plump, and dressed casually in slacks and suede shirt, without make-up. (2)............... In fact she has built up her daughter's career since 25 she was eleven months old and appeared in a soap commercial.

Who is the real Brooke Shields? Sexy teenage siren or a sweet romantic girl? 30 (3)............... All of these? Or none? There are two keys to Brooke's personality: her looks and her mother.

(4)............... She inherited the 35 Shields looks and athleticism, being an excellent rider and an all-round athlete. Her father is now an executive with a consulting firm, living in Manhattan with his second wife Didi. 40

Brooke's mother, born Teri Schmon, is from a poor and devout Roman Catholic background. At 31 she was managing a small restaurant when 45 handsome Frank Shields walked in one night. (5)...............

Teri Schmon Shields has worked all her life, and so has Brooke. (6)............... Since 1980 50 their average yearly income has been $1 million. Brooke Shields and Company has only one product: Brooke Shields.

Not surprisingly, Brooke is 55 shy with strangers. She is serious about her studies at Princeton, and quite brainy. (7)...............

Brooke is unwavering in her 60 ambition to become an even better film star. When she talks about acting she gets interested and comes across as a very nice girl who would really like 65 to get to grips with her profession.

At eighteen, will Brookie, as her friends call her, now come out of her shell, assert her own 70 personality – which is really very appealing – and then go on to real acting, unafraid to show her emotions? (8)...............

(Rosemary Wittman Lamb in the *Sunday Express Magazine*)

15

Dealing with unfamiliar words

In units 1 and 2, we looked at two techniques to help you guess the general sense of unfamiliar words. But often you can understand the general sense of a sentence or the passage as a whole without knowing what every word means. These techniques may help you.

Decide whether you need to understand the exact meaning of the unfamiliar word in order to understand the general sense of the sentence or the passage.

Decide what part of speech the word is.

Look in the context for clues to its general sense.

Read on and confirm or revise your guess.

1 The following sentences are taken from the passage, but in each one there is one word missing. Without looking back at the passage, think of suitable words to fill the blanks.
   Write down any word which you think might fill in the blank.
   Example: a) skin, texture, complexion.

   a) 'And that famous face! A .... like honey and cream.'
   b) 'Green eyes skilfully made up that .... at you bright and clear.'
   c) 'Who is the real Brooke Shields? Sexy teenage .... or a sweet romantic girl?'
   d) 'Brooke's height and looks come from her father's side. She .... the Shields looks and athleticism.'
   e) 'She is serious about her studies and quite ....'
   f) 'Will Brookie (. . .) now come out of her ...., assert her own personality?'

   Look at the passage to check whether you guessed correctly. If the word you guessed wasn't exactly the word in the passage, read on and decide whether it means more or less the same.

2 There may be other words in the passage which you don't understand. Use the four techniques to guess their general meaning.

Inferring

Work in pairs. Discuss what evidence there is in the passage for the following statements.

a) The writer thinks Brooke is attractive.
Example: a) The writer thinks Brooke is attractive because he describes her as 'a sexy teenage siren'. (line 28)

b) Brooke's looks do not come from her mother.
c) Brooke's mother is a competent business woman.
d) Brooke does not live with her father.
e) Brooke is not quite grown up yet.
f) Brooke is firmly controlled by her mother.

Further work

1 Work in pairs.
   Student A: You are a famous person, such as a film star or a sportsman/woman, who began work as a child. Tell Student B who you are. Prepare a short biography of yourself. You may choose a real person; if so, use reference books to help you prepare your autobiography.
   Student B: You are a journalist who is going to interview a famous person who began work as a child. Ask Student A who he/she is. You have strong views about the exploitation of children. Prepare the questions you wish to ask during the interview. You may use reference books to help you learn something about the person before the interview.
   When you are both ready, carry out the interview.

2 Think about all the people who have influenced you strongly in your life. Can you imagine what might have happened or what you might have done without this influence? Prepare a short autobiography which describes their influence on you, and tell your partner about it.

3 Look back over the passage and if you have read them, the passages in units 1 and 2. Note down twenty words or expressions which you have learnt. Using as much of this new vocabulary as possible, write a paragraph on one of the following subjects:

   – How others see me.
   – 'The best friendships are made from conflicting personalities.' Discuss.
   – Describe family life in your country.
   – Do you think children are ever commercially exploited?

Unit 4   The good picnic guide

Extracting main ideas

Read the passage opposite and then answer the questions below.

Which of the following definitions of a picnic would the writer be likely to choose?

a) A fashionable social entertainment in which each party present contributes a share of the provisions to be eaten outdoors.
b) A feast of carefully prepared food and wines to be enjoyed with friends and particularly children in the country.
c) A quick snack to be eaten during a short stop on a long journey.
d) A meal eaten outdoors on a sunny day in the country surrounded by children who are allowed to do whatever they wish.
e) A lunchtime party in a country field that is reasonably safe for children.

Inferring

Work in pairs. Discuss what evidence there is in the passage for the following statements. If there is no evidence, explain what the passage really says.

a) The writer dislikes picnics where there are too many things to carry.
Example: a) True; the writer dislikes picnics where there are too many things to carry because he gives a long list of things *not* to take on a picnic (lines 15–22), and because he suggests that the children should carry their own food and drink (lines 68–9), and he also suggests that when you leave you will have nothing to carry (lines 101–106).

b) The Japanese like formal picnics.
c) The writer thinks children can be useful as servants on picnics.
d) On picnics, children must be allowed to be as free as possible.
e) The food must be attractive and tasty rather than nutritious.
f) The picnic site should be exciting and slightly dangerous for the children.
g) The writer doesn't like sandwiches on picnics.
h) The best picnics are ones when you and the children feel sick afterwards.

18

The subject is picnics. Please take notes, and smoke if you wish. We will kick off by defining not what a picnic is, but what a picnic is not.

5   A picnic is not a feast of cold chicken, tomato salad, pickles, tongue, ham and warmish white wine consumed off a damask tablecloth in a field, wood or spinney.

10   Such a meal is only a portable business lunch, eaten at a table without legs and thus – unless you happen to be Japanese – liable to give you indigestion. Anyway, you've forgotten the mayonnaise.

15   A picnic is not sandwiches. Nor is it vacuum-flasks and greaseproof-paper bags in a car parked on a cliff top with the windows up.

Nor is it hampers, spirit kettles, portable
20   barbecues, collapsible stools, storm-proof field-ovens or any other kind of Ideal Home Exhibition alfresco gadgetry.

What, then, is a picnic?

The following elements are indispens-
25   able:

ONE: Children. A picnic without children is like roast beef without York-shire pudding. Children are the whole delight and purpose of a picnic, as well as
30   coming in useful for fetching cigarettes.

TWO: Glorious weather. This is vital, for picnics and mackintoshes do not go hand in hand. Picnics were intended to be eaten under a blue sky, with wasps in
35   attendance.

THREE: A good site. There is a lot more in this than finding a meadow with fine, springy grass and its fair ration of buttercups. There must be streams to fall
40   in, trees to fall out of, hills to roll down, and preferably a mad bull somewhere in the offing. This gives picnicking its proper air of adventure.

FOUR: The right food. The following
45   recipe is culled from a lifetime's experience and will yield a successful picnic for four people.

You get four small deep carrier bags of the kind that are used by wine merchants
50   to hold one bottle of Scotch.

Into each carrier bag you place these ingredients:

One banana. One orange. One small portion of processed cheese. One handful
55   of assorted biscuits, plain and sweet. One packet of chewing gum. One sausage roll. One bag of potato crisps. One hard-boiled egg. Some cheese straws. A screw-top bottle of fizzy lemonade. One gingerbread man. One bun. One bar of chocolate. One 60 stick of barley sugar.

And other items to taste, provided that they are not boringly wholesome, that they were not left over from yesterday's dinner and especially that they are not 65 placed between two slices of bread, whether brown or white.

You hand out the carrier bags to your squad of picnickers and you set off.

You do not worry if the oldest one, who 70 has been crazed with hunger ever since finishing breakfast ten minutes ago, commences to eat his picnic before the car is even out of the garage.

You do not worry if the youngest one 75 eats his chocolate before he gets to his sausage roll, or even if he eats his sausage roll at all.

You do not worry about your children getting sticky.   80

You do not worry about your children feeling sick.

You do not, in fact, worry about any-thing. You park the car and step out briskly into the countryside. You find a 85 suitable spot. You sit down. You act as arbitrator while your children set up a brisk barter trade in boiled eggs and bananas.

You eat. Your children begin to eat, 90 cease eating in order to catch dragonflies and resume eating after they have fallen in a bog.

You do not warn them against germs or about indigestion.   95

You light a cigarette.

The sun shines on.

You fall asleep. All is rustic and peaceful except for the occasional magic cries of small picnickers being stung by wasps.   100

When it is time to leave, you heave your discarded carrier bags into the nearest litter bin and return home unencumbered by rugs, vacuum-flasks or wicker shopping baskets containing milk bottles and un- 105 wanted bread.

You will feel bloated and dyspeptic for your picnic will have been stodgy, messy and almost totally lacking in vitamins. But it will have contained the one ingredient 110 that no successful picnic can afford to be without.

It will have been memorable, I promise you.

(Keith Waterhouse: *Mondays Thursdays*)

Understanding writer's style

1 Answer the following questions.

a) The author writes: 'The subject is picnics. Please take notes, and smoke if you wish.' (lines 1–2) to create the impression that he is:
   i)   giving a lecture.
   ii) writing a newspaper article.
   iii) talking to his children.

b) 'A picnic without children is like roast beef without Yorkshire pudding.' (lines 26–8) suggests that the writer:
   i) always eats Yorkshire pudding with roast beef.
   ii) sometimes eats roast beef with Yorkshire pudding.

c) 'Picnics were intended to be eaten under a blue sky, with wasps in attendance.' (lines 33–5) suggests that:
   i) unfortunately you can't get rid of wasps on picnics.
   ii) the perfect picnic ironically involves a little discomfort.

d) 'You do not worry if the oldest one. . .' (lines 70–4) suggests that:
   i) older children need more to eat.
   ii) the writer is amused by how much children can eat.

e) 'Your children begin to eat. . .' (lines 90–3) suggests that:
   i) on the perfect picnic, children are allowed to do as they please, whatever the consequences.
   ii) children do not usually eat all their lunch in one go.

Check your answers with another student.

2 The writer uses humour in the passage to convey his argument. Underline any sentences which you think are meant to be humorous. Then decide whether you think the humour is successful or not. Ask your partner what he or she thinks.

Writing summaries

Writing an effective summary involves presenting the main points of a passage as concisely and as accurately as possible.

1 Decide whether the following statements accurately represent the main points in the passage.

a) Choose a picnic site which is not only attractive but also interesting for the children.
b) Make the children wait until lunchtime before they start eating.

   c) Make sure the four most important elements are present: children, good weather, a good site and the right food.

   d) Roast beef and Yorkshire pudding are indispensable.

   e) Put all the food in individual bags so you do not have to carry it all.

   f) Don't make the picnic too formal.

   g) Don't forget to take cooking utensils as the best food for picnics is cooked outdoors.

   h) Business lunches outdoors are not very comfortable.

   i) If you want a memorable picnic, make sure the food is nutritious.

   j) Prepare all the food before you leave.

   k) Tidy up before you leave the picnic site.

   l) Try not to be too strict with the children.

  m) Make sure the children don't get up to any mischief.

2 Now re-order all the accurate statements according to their position in the passage. These statements now form the 'skeleton' of a summary.

3 Look at the inaccurate statements. Decide whether they contain main points. If so, re-write them and place them in a suitable position in the skeleton.

4 Now re-read the passage and check whether any of the important information has been left out. If it has, re-write the relevant statement to include it.

Further work

Work in groups of two or three. Using at least ten words from the passage, discuss which are the most important elements for your perfect picnic. Choose five of them.

Now ask other groups whether they have the same ideas for the perfect picnic as you. Try and organise a picnic that will appeal to as many people in the class as possible. Think about food, site, transport, other people to invite etc.

Unit 5   Down and Out in Paris and London

This passage is taken from a book by George Orwell called *Down and Out in Paris and London*, which was first published in 1933. It describes the writer's experiences when he was trying to live on very little money.

Understanding text organisation

Read the passage slowly. There are six sentences in the passage which have been printed in the wrong position.
For example: 'They are part of the process of being hard up' should go after '. . .on six francs a day.' (line 43)
Decide which are the other five sentences that have been printed in the wrong position, and where they should go.

Inferring

Decide whether there is any evidence in the passage for the following statements. If there is, note it down.

a)   The writer was forced to lie about his poverty.
b)   There was no proper kitchen in the house where the writer lived.
c)   The writer deliberately flicked the bug into the milk.
d)   He was more concerned about hygiene than about eating.
e)   He was ashamed of admitting that he didn't have any money.
f)   Bread was sold by weight rather than by the loaf.
g)   Bakers' girls usually tried to overcharge customers.
h)   Going to the bakers' shops required a great deal of courage.
i)   He was ashamed that the greengrocer might have thought he was deliberately trying to pay with a Belgian coin.
j)   He was jealous of his rich friends.
k)   Bread and margarine was not very filling.
l)   He didn't take the bread because he thought it was wrong to steal.
m) Being bored made him hungry.
n)   Most people in Paris were either very rich or had no money at all.

You discover the extreme precariousness of your six francs a day. Mean disasters happen and rob you of food. You have spent your last eighty centimes on half a litre of milk, and are boiling it over the spirit lamp. While it boils a bug runs down your forearm; you give the bug a flick with your nail, and it falls, plop! straight into the milk. It is hours before you dare venture into a baker's shop again.

You go to the baker's to buy a pound of bread, and you wait while the girl cuts a pound for another customer. She is clumsy, and cuts more than a pound. *'Pardon, monsieur,'* she says, 'I suppose you don't mind paying two sous extra?' When you think that you too might be asked to pay two sous extra, and would have to confess that you could not, you bolt in panic. There is nothing for it but to throw the milk away and go foodless.

You go to the greengrocer's to spend a franc on a kilogram of potatoes. Bread is a franc a pound, and you have exactly a franc. But one of the pieces that make up the franc is a Belgian piece, and the shopman refuses it. You slink out of the shop, and can never go there again.

You have strayed into a respectable quarter, and you see a prosperous friend coming. For half a day at a time you lie on your bed, feeling like the *jeune squelette* in Baudelaire's poem. To avoid him you dodge into the nearest café. Once in the café you must buy something, so you spend your last fifty centimes on a glass of black coffee with a dead fly in it. With bread and margarine in your belly, you go out and look into the shop windows. One could multiply these disasters by the hundred.

You discover what it is like to be hungry. Everywhere there is food insulting you in huge wasteful piles; whole dead pigs, baskets of hot loaves, great yellow blocks of butter, strings of sausages, mountains of potatoes, vast Gruyère cheeses like grindstones. A snivelling self-pity comes over you at the sight of so much food. They are part of the process of being hard up. You plan to grab a loaf and run, swallowing it before they catch you; and you refrain, from pure funk.

You discover the boredom which is inseparable from poverty; the times when you have nothing to do and, being underfed, can interest yourself in nothing. Only food could rouse you. You discover that a man who has gone even a week on bread and margarine is not a man any longer, only a belly with a few accessory organs.

This – one could describe it further, but it is all in the same style – is life on six francs a day. Thousands of people in Paris live it – struggling artists and students, prostitutes when their luck is out, out-of-work people of all kinds. It is the suburbs, as it were, of poverty.

(George Orwell: *Down and Out in Paris and London*)

Dealing with unfamiliar words

1 Very often you can find clues to the meaning of unfamiliar words in their immediate context. Sometimes the clues are fairly obvious.

Look at the following verbs in the passage and decide whether they mean *enter* or *leave*.

a) 'venture' (line 6)
b) 'bolt' (line 13)
c) 'slink' (line 18)
d) 'strayed' (line 20)
e) 'dodge' (line 23)

Which words helped you make up your mind?

2 To get a better idea of what the words mean, you may have to make use of clues which are less obvious.

The exact meaning of each of the words above can be explained by adding an *adverb* or *adverbial phrase* to *enter* or *leave*. Choose the best answer to the questions below.

a) 'venture': After the experience in the baker's, you no longer have the courage to go into the shop for some time. Venture means to *enter/leave* (i) hesitantly, (ii) boldly, (iii) happily.
b) 'bolt': You are so afraid that you might be asked to pay two sous extra that you *enter/leave* (i) quickly, (ii) slowly, (iii) bravely.
c) 'slink': You feel that you can never go to the greengrocer's again after he has refused one of your coins. So you *enter/leave* (i) proudly, (ii) full of shame, (iii) angrily.
d) 'strayed': You are very poor and probably badly dressed, so you *enter/leave* the respectable quarter (i) on purpose, (ii) in a relaxed fashion, (iii) by mistake.
e) 'dodge': You see your friend coming, and you want to avoid him. You *enter/leave* the café (i) slowly, (ii) quickly, (iii) playfully.

3 There may be some other words or expressions which you don't understand. Choose six or seven and use the techniques explained above and in units 1, 2 and 3 to guess their general sense. When you have finished you can check their meaning in your dictionary.

Linking ideas

Answer the following questions.

a) '. . .and it falls plop! straight into the milk.' (lines 5–6)
   What does?
b) 'I suppose you don't mind paying two sous extra?' (line 11)
   How much is the girl asking for the bread?
c) '. . .and would have to confess that you could not. . .' (line 13)
   Could not what?
d) 'One could multiply these disasters by the hundred.' (lines 26–7)
   What disasters?
e) 'This – one could describe it further. . .' (line 42)
   Describe what further?
f) 'It is the suburbs. . .' (line 45)
   What is?

Further work

1 Think about how much you spend on food a day, and what you buy. Form
   groups of four or five and compare notes. Who spends the most and who spends
   the least?
      Now decide how much it would cost you to buy just enough food to live on
   per day. Discuss exactly what you would buy with it, and whether you'd enjoy
   living like this. Compare your notes with other groups.
      If you're in a class with people from different countries, find out which
   country is the most expensive to live in, and which is the cheapest when you have
   very little money. If you're in a class with people from your own country, find
   out which countries would be cheaper to live in.

2 In many countries, such as in Asia and Africa, food costs comparatively little but
   people are still starving. Work in groups of two or three. Choose a very poor
   country and compare the standard of living there with that of your own country.
   Try and decide how this country could be helped.

3 Using at least ten words and expressions from this passage, write a paragraph
   describing what happened when the writer finally had a proper meal.

Unit 6   A family lunch in Beirut

Understanding text organisation

The sentences printed below have all been taken from the passage opposite.
Read the passage through and then decide where they should go.

a) The days of low prices are a distant memory.

b) In a sense, the Friday gathering is more than just a family meal for the Saidi clan, it is a celebration of their survival from week to week.

c) As the lunch hour approaches, members of the family begin to arrive.

d) This delights Mme Saidi, whose pleasure in cooking is to see her family together, enjoying the meal.

e) Today, I am sorry to say, we have no fish, because it has become too expensive.

f) In the Arab world, Friday is the 'sabbath' and the natural time for family socialising.

g) Cold drinks are served, fruit juice and nothing stronger than Lebanese beer.

h) From courgettes, ten different dishes.

Extracting main ideas

Choose a suitable title for the passage from the list below.

- Lunchtime in Lebanon.
- Celebrating survival over the dinner table.
- The flavour and imagination of Lebanese cooking.
- Feeding a hungry family.

Eight years of civil war in Lebanon, of shooting and shelling and bombing, have not deterred the Saidi family from gathering around the table of Mme Saidi, the 72-year-old matriarch of the clan, for the customary Friday lunch. And from the busy activity in Mme Saidi's kitchen, the iron pots bubbling on the stove, the cornucopia of fresh vegetables on the kitchen table, the aroma of herbs and spices, garlic and peppers, you would not know that Beirut was still a beleaguered city, or that the population of this once enchanting Mediterranean paradise still lives under the pressures of random violence and dangerous uncertainty.

It is a mark of the resilience and the determination of the Lebanese and of families like the Saidis that they have been able to maintain a semblance of normal life and family customs.

Today's meal is to be a feast of many traditional Lebanese dishes: kibbinayeh (a tartare-like dish of raw ground mutton with ground wheat and spices), kibbeh meshweh (balls of grilled meat fat, walnuts, spices and onions), 'mjederah (cooked lentils, fried onions and ground wheat, lbnimu (a cooked yoghurt sauce with meat and onions), mnezeleh (a casserole-like dish of cooked aubergines, onions, houmous, tomatoes, green peppers, garlic and olive oil), fareek (ground wheat), a chicken and macaroni dish in a milk sauce and salad, followed by melon and fresh fruit and a choice of five flavours of ice cream and sherbet.

Lebanese cooking is flavourful and imaginative. From four or five basic things, Mme Saidi points out, the Lebanese make 50 different dishes. From lentils, perhaps five varieties of soup and half a dozen variations of 'mjederah. From aubergines, more than ten.

The troubles in Lebanon over the past eight years have, inevitably, made some ingredients of Lebanese cooking scarce and others prohibitively expensive.

'I keep books,' says Mme Saidi, 'and I find things have gone up more than 100 times. Meat was difficult the past few years and fresh meat is still expensive. Most of our lamb comes from Turkey, the beef from Europe. It can cost as much as 50 Lebanese pounds (£8) per kilo. A red fish we like, sultan ibrahim, costs 150 Lebanese pounds (£25) for one kilo.'

Mme Saidi makes quick forays out of the kitchen to greet them with hugs and kisses, warm welcomes, then hurries back to watch over the cooking.

It has just gone 2.30 pm and everyone is together. Baskets full of flat, round Lebanese bread are passed around. The food comes not so much in courses, starters, main dishes, but in waves of flavours. Everyone helps themselves.

Plates are filled and refilled. The many dishes, family favourites, the kibbinayeh, kibbeh meshweh, and 'mjederah, all so carefully and painstakingly prepared, disappear as if by a conjuror's trick. So that for a while at least, on Friday afternoons, the troubles of their country can be put aside and the illusion of normal life, of laughter and living well can go on.

(James Horowitz in the *Mail on Sunday YOU Magazine*)

Dealing with unfamiliar words

1 In unit 5 we saw how you can sometimes find clues to the meaning of unfamiliar words in their immediate context. But sometimes you also have to look for clues elsewhere in the passage.

For example: 'beleaguered' (line 13)

'Eight years of civil war in Lebanon. . .' (line 1)

'. . .still lives under the pressures of random violence. . .' (lines 16–17)

We know that there had been a civil war in the Lebanon for eight years when this passage was written. We also know that the city 'still lives under the pressure of random violence. . .' 'Beleaguered' must be a negative characteristic of life in Beirut at the time. So it might mean something like 'under attack'.

You may not understand the words and expressions in the left hand column. Use the clues in the right hand column to help you work out what they might mean.

a) *'matriarch* of the *clan'* (lines 6–7): 'Mme Saidi . . . 72-year-old. . .' (line 5) '. . .the Saidi family. . .' (line 3)

b) *'customary* Friday lunch' (lines 6–7): '. . .the Friday gathering. . .' (sentence b) '. . .the natural time for family socialising.' (sentence f)

c) *'cornucopia* of fresh vegetables' (line 9): 'Today's meal is to be a feast of many. . .dishes.' (lines 25–6)

d) *'resilience'* (line 19): '. . .shooting and shelling and bombing. . .' (line 2) '. . .the troubles of their country can be put aside. . .' (lines 87–8)

Check your answers with another student. Do you both agree on the meanings of these words and expressions?
   When you have finished you can check your guesses by looking the words up in a dictionary.

2 There may still be some words which you don't understand. Choose four and try to work out what they mean by using the techniques explained in unit 3. Write down what you think they mean.
   Check with another student. Does he/she have the same words as you? Do you both agree on the meaning? Discuss the words which only appear on one list.

Reading for specific information

1 Look through the passage again and find five basic ingredients of Lebanese cooking.
2 Name these recipes for two of the dishes mentioned in the passage.

a) Approx. 4½ cups of ground wheat
1 leg of mutton
3 medium onions
1 red pepper
1 teaspoon of mixed spices
½ teaspoon of cinnamon
iced water
salt, pepper to taste

Wash the ground wheat and drain. Remove the meat from the bone and the fat and gristle from the meat. Grind it twice, and then grind the onions and red pepper. Knead them into the meat, with the seasoning and the spices, and then knead in the ground wheat, adding an occasional tablespoon of iced water to keep the mixture smooth. Refrigerate for 6–12 hours. This is the basic kibbeh mix. Mould the mixture into small oval shapes and arrange on a plate with fresh mint. Serve with olive oil and raw onion.

b) 1 kilo of stewing meat, in large pieces
8 small white onions, peeled
1 cinnamon stick
2½ cups of yoghurt cooked slowly with an egg white and cornflour
2 cloves of garlic
1 tablespoon of clarified butter
1 teaspoon of ground coriander

Place the meat and onions in a saucepan, and add seasoning and cinammon. Cover with water, bring to the boil, cover and simmer until tender and most of the water has evaporated. Remove the cinammon stick. Bring the yoghurt to the boil and, stirring well, add to the meat and onions. Simmer for 15 minutes. Crush the garlic with a little salt. Fry it in the clarified butter with the coriander. Stir into stew. Serve hot with rice or ground wheat.

Further work

1 Prepare a recipe for a traditional dish from your country. Include all the ingredients and instructions on how to make it. You can use the recipes above as a model for the instructions.
2 If you're in a class with people from different countries, choose a partner from a country other than your own. Find out about a traditional meal in his or her country and prepare a short description of it, comparing it to a similar meal in your own country.
3 Look back over this passage and, if you have read them, the passages in units 4 and 5. Write down twenty useful words and expressions which you have learnt. Using as much of the new vocabulary as possible, write a paragraph on one of the following subjects:
     – Describe the best meal you have ever had.
     – How to eat cheaply.
     – How do you think famine relief in countries where there is starvation and drought could be better organised?

Unit 7   House for sale

Checking comprehension

1 Look at these pictures of houses for sale. Match them with their descriptions.

1

2

3

4

A CLAPHAM - LONDON SW4 A superb, deceptively spacious, particularly well-modernised Victorian terraced house of great charm, just south of the river. Close to Clapham Common Underground. 2 large double bedrooms, sitting room, kitchen/dining area. Utility room at end of 45' south-facing garden.

B ESSEX - near DUNMOW A most attractive home of great character set in large well-maintained gardens, with swimming pool and hard tennis court. 3/4 reception rooms, 6 bedrooms, 2 garages, nuclear air raid shelter. Brand new kitchen, solar heating.

C SOUTH KENSINGTON - LONDON Spacious 3-storey Victorian house in need of some redecoration. 1st floor drawing room with balcony over communal gardens. Roof terrace, large double garage. Electric central heating. Price includes carpets, curtains and kitchen equipment.

D ALDWICH - WEST SUSSEX A modern detached family house, close to the sea. 24' living room and extension. Large windows with excellent view of the sea. Newly modernised kitchen, 3 bedrooms. Landscaped garden, garage, thermal insulation. BUILT 1981.

E BELGRAVIA - LONDON SW1 Charming period terraced house on 3 floors with extremely pretty garden. Hall, drawing room, cloakroom. Gas central heating. Caretaker. Inspection recommended. LEASE - 99 years.

F MAIDSTONE - KENT Quietly situated, detached, luxury bungalow set in 2½ acres of ground adjoining fields at rear. Garden study and heated swimming pool. Oil-fired central heating. 3 bedrooms, bathroom, shower room. Extension on to landscaped terrace. BUILT 10 YEARS AGO.

2 Choose one of the houses and imagine that you are the owner. What would be the advantages and disadvantages for you of living in this house? Note down your ideas.

3 Find another student who has chosen the same house as you have, and discuss your ideas.

31

Extracting main ideas

1 Each of the paragraphs in the following passage refers to different features of the house, which are numbered in the illustration. Match the numbered features in the illustration to the corresponding paragraphs.

A Central heating: gas-fired systems are the kind everybody wants. Electric central heating is being aggressively marketed – but the industry's bold claims of remarkably small bills are based on consumption in super-insulated houses built within the last five years. Electric heating in a 30-year-old house is bad news. Oil-fired systems are also expensive to operate and, where there is no option of converting to gas, they act as a similar deterrent to buyers.

B Double glazing – its only real value is to cut noise nuisance, as heat savings are so limited that it will be years before initial cash outlay is recouped.

C Garden improvements: so expensive, you benefit largely while you live in the house. Good gardens don't put much on resale value.

D First garage: much more influential on resale price than second or third garage. Compare costs carefully of matching the garage to blend with existing brickwork of the house or of investing in concrete prefab design which will stand away from house.

E Modernising and updating fixtures and fittings; an attractive kitchen may well sell the house: but the astronomical price of modern kitchen units is unlikely to be recouped on resale.

F Nuclear air-raid shelter; you might get a loan if your mortgage is only a small percentage of property value. But not enough buyers are sufficiently worried by prospect of nuclear war to push up prices of properties with shelters.

G Bathroom/inside toilet: a particularly good improvement (especially when done with improvement grant from local authority) if in an extension to house, for instance in the "back addition". A bathroom/inside toilet might not add much to the value of a property if it replaces an existing bedroom, thereby cutting down sleeping accommodation.

H Thermal insulation and improvements to the heating system: these may lower your fuel bills, but they won't put much on eventual resale price.

I Solar heating: it's always about to arrive as a great technical breakthrough, but never quite does. Might help a bit to warm the water in the swimming-pool.

J Increased accommodation and living area: the trick here is to use the existing walls and layout of the house to cut down your building cost. Typical example is the bedroom which can be slotted in above a garage or a single-storey part of the house. To be most productive in terms of resale value, extra living space should be attached to the house. Garden study is all very well, but nothing like so attractive to potential purchasers if it is sited beyond the potato patch.

K Replacement windows: may provide a nice garden view, but basically are no more than a repair, and a purchaser won't pay much more on account of them.

L Swimming-pool: most people fight shy of maintenance costs.

(Jeremy Gates in the
Sunday Express Magazine)

2 Complete the table below by listing the improvements which will add value to a
property, and those that won't.

Improvements which add value	Improvements which don't add value
gas-fired central heating	electric/oil-fired central heating

Reading for specific information

The passage describes the effects of home improvements on the price of houses when they are sold. Imagine that you want to sell the house you chose in *Checking comprehension* 2. Look through the passage quickly and decide which features of the house will help you sell it for a high price, and which might discourage potential buyers.

Understanding text organisation

1 Some of the home improvements which will add value to the house have certain conditions attached to them.
   For example: A first garage will add value *as long as* it matches the existing
   brickwork or stands away from the house.
   Complete the following sentences with information from the passage, using words like: *if, as long as, provided (that), assuming (that).*

   a) Everyone wants central heating. . .
   b) Oil-fired central heating might be acceptable to buyers. . .
   c) You can increase accommodation and living area cheaply. . .
   d) Bathroom and toilet improvements are attractive. . .

2 Some of the home improvements which won't add value still have certain advantages.
   For example: Thermal insulation won't add any value to the house *although* it
   may lower fuel bills.
   Complete the following sentences with information from the passage using words like: *but, although.*

   a) Solar heating is not particularly attractive to buyers. . .
   b) Electric central heating is economical in new houses. . .
   c) Cutting noise nuisance is double glazing's real value. . .
   d) It is true that garden improvements are very attractive. . .

Further work

1 Work in groups of two or three. This unit has dealt with some of the factors which can influence home buyers. What other factors are there?
   Think about transport, local schools, traffic, shopping facilities.
   Draw up a list of the factors in order of priority. Discuss your list with a neighbouring group and draw up a new list of priorities. Then present your conclusions to the rest of the class.

2 Draw a plan and write a short description of your own home using at least ten
   words and expressions from the passage. Include features which would attract
   buyers as well as those which would discourage them. When you are ready, look
   at your partner's description. Prepare a short advertisement for his/her home.
   Place the advertisement in a position where everyone can see it. Try and sell your
   partner's home to someone else in the class, and buy a new home.

Unit 8 Burgled seven times

Predicting

1 Look at the title of the unit. Think of ten to fifteen words which you are likely to find in the passage.
2 Working with another student, think of five things you can do to prevent burglaries.
3 Now read the passage and check whether the words you predicted in 1 actually appeared.

Understanding text organisation

SHE'S well known in the local glass merchants. "Oh, you ain't been done *again*, 'ave you?" they cry, as Fel Watkins walks
5 in, because intruders have broken into her Clapham flat seven times in the space of 16 months.

During this period, only one
10 of the other 21 flats in her block has been burgled; and the previous occupant of her flat lived there for 40 years, without being burgled once.
15 She has realised the place is everything the burglars love. It's on the ground floor, set back from the road, with a good screen of trees and bushes, and
20 plenty of easy exits over walls to common land and to the railway line.

She decided to treat the experience as a lesson, to get the
25 crime prevention officer round and carry out the improvements to security which he suggested.

"That was my biggest," she
30 said. "I had a girl-friend living here and between us we lost every bit of jewellery we had and three watches, cameras and a cassette player."

"There was a phone call at 35 half past 11 at night. It was my neighbour who said: 'There's something funny going on in your flat, and all the lights are on.' I was really upset this time. 40 I felt so helpless I just burst into tears. That was the first time I'd cried about it all."

At this point she wrote to her MP, saying that she knew what 45 she was doing trying to keep these people out of her home and that she'd like to know what he was doing. He wrote back, blaming unemployment, 50 which Fel says she "sort of believes".

After the fourth break-in, the police, at their own expense, connected an alarm, which 55 would ring at the police station but not in the flat.

The crime prevention officers had told Fel that there was no problem with the small window 60 above the kitchen door, as it was less than nine inches

36

across. But three boys managed to squeeze through.
65 The police saw them but they ran off down the railway line.

"Although nothing was taken, they turned the place upside down, which happened
70 in each case except the sixth and seventh," said Fel. The sixth time an attempt was made the police charged a man.

Fel was asked by the police if
75 anyone bore her a grudge. "I had the feeling that everyone in Clapham was checking me out," she said. "But the police said that it didn't work that
80 way. They said it wasn't natural to suffer like this, so they thought it was a vendetta."

She discovered she wasn't the most burgled person local-
85 ly: that was a magistrate living near Clapham Common who has been burgled 18 times in two years.

After the first few incidents, Fel admits that she was in a 90 terrible state of shock, that her heart would be pounding every time she got back from the office, wondering what she'd find, and that she slept very 95 lightly.

Now she manages to sleep but is very jumpy about walking around the local streets.

"That would have been a real 100 clean-up job. But the alarm went off as the burglars tried the sitting room. They had piled everything up outside the kitchen door, including the hi-fi 105 with all its wires cut."

"As I was coming back from work, I saw a collection of neighbours outside my door and I instantly knew what had 110 happened. There was silence as I approached. Then someone said, "You've been done again."

(Jane Roberts in *The Standard*)

The following sentences have all been removed from the passage. Decide where they should go.

a) The first break-in, which was also her first burglary in 12 years of living in London, happened only six weeks after she moved in.

b) In spite of all this, nine days after the first, she suffered her second burglary.

c) The third happened while Fel, a secretary, was staying with her mother in Hampshire.

d) It was there in plenty of time for the fifth break-in, when it was set off by the intruders.

e) Of the seventh (and last so far), Fel says:

Checking comprehension

Decide whether the following statements are true, false, or whether you don't know according to the passage.

a) The burglars usually got into Fel Watkins' flat by breaking a window.
b) There are few burglaries in Clapham.
c) Fel Watkins has been very unlucky to be burgled so often.
d) The flat is well-protected against burglaries because of its location.
e) She forgot to ask a neighbour to keep an eye on the flat.
f) Most burglars are unemployed.
g) The police paid for certain improvements to security in Fel's flat.
h) She's scared that she'll be burgled while she's at home.
i) She lost most of her belongings in the seventh burglary.

Understanding complex sentences

Look at the following sentences and punctuate them. Do not look back at the text. It may help you to read them aloud.

a) It's on the ground floor set back from the road with a good screen of trees and bushes and plenty of easy exits over walls to common land and to the railway line.
b) The first break-in which was also her first burglary in 12 years of living in London happened only six weeks after she moved in.
c) After the fourth break-in the police at their own expense connected an alarm which would ring at the police station but not in the flat.
d) After the first few incidents Fel admits that she was in a terrible state of shock that her heart would be pounding every time she got back from the office wondering what she'd find and that she slept very lightly.

Writing summaries

1 Look at the following document which is issued by the Metropolitan Police, London. Imagine you are a Crime Prevention Officer. Write down five questions you would ask a householder about his/her property if they had asked you for advice on how to beat the burglar.
2 Work in pairs. Ask your partner the questions you prepared about his or her house/flat, and answer questions about yours.
3 Write a brief report giving your advice as Crime Prevention Officer on how you would make your partner's home more secure against burglary.

Beat the Burglar

Don't invite crime – take basic, sensible precautions. Your house and property are valuable and must be properly protected. When you buy a lock, you buy time – and this is the one thing a burglar can't afford. Most thieves are casual opportunists to whom the best deterrents are delay and noise which could mean discovery.

When you leave it – lock it!

First of all, fit security locks to all doors and windows and a safety chain on the front door. Secondly, use them! And use them every time you go out, even if it's only for a short time. If you have any ladders or tools, don't leave them lying about in the garden, lock them away or at least immobilise them. Don't rely on "safe" or "secret" places for keys and valuables – nine times out of ten, they are the first place a thief will look.

When you move house ....

When you move into a new home, even if it is fitted with security locks, change them. You don't know who may have duplicate keys. When you are new to a district, you are particularly vulnerable. Never let anyone that you don't know into your house. An official-looking cap is not enough, ask for proof of identity and look at it carefully – if you are still not satisfied, don't let the person in.

Valuables need special protection

Really valuable items, such as jewellery, should be given special protection – preferably by leaving them with your bank. But a small security safe, properly installed, should protect you against all but the most determined burglar. It is also most important to maintain an up-to-date list of valuables and their descriptions. In the case of fine art, paintings, ceramics or jewellery, colour photographs can sometimes be of assistance to the police should you be unfortunate enough to have them stolen. Enter the details on the back of the pictures. But don't keep such documents in your house, keep them at the bank or with your insurance company.

Going on holiday?

Don't advertise the fact that your house is empty. Do remember to cancel the milk and newspapers and also to draw curtains back. Don't leave notes for tradesmen and try not to talk about your holidays and future plans loudly in public. Operate a "Good Neighbour" scheme to ensure that mail is taken in, the house checked regularly and that lights are put on. If you plan to be away for a long time, make sure that your lawn is cut. Call at your local police station and tell them you are going away. Make sure that they know who has your spare key and how you can be contacted in case of trouble. Especially at holiday time, don't leave cash or valuables in the house – take them with you or lodge them with the bank.

(Metropolitan Police: *Beat the Burglar*)

Further work

1   Are there many burglaries in the area where you live? Fel Watkins' Member of Parliament blames unemployment for the number of burglaries. Do you agree? With your partner, make a list of all the factors which increase the risk of burglary. Think of social, economic and political aspects of the problem. Discuss your views with the rest of the class.
2   Walk round your school. Are there any recommendations you could make to increase security against burglary? Working in pairs, prepare a brief report and then present your conclusions to the rest of the class.

Unit 9   Sissinghurst Castle

Sissinghurst Castle is an old house with a beautiful garden in Kent, England. The main buildings date from the sixteenth century, although parts of it are much older. It was bought and restored in the 1930s by Vita Sackville-West, the writer, and her husband, Harold Nicholson.

Extracting main ideas

Read the description of Sissinghurst and choose a suitable title for each paragraph from the list below. Use the map to help you.

a) The Library
b) The Rose Garden
c) The Tower Lawn
d) The Cottage Garden
e) The Tower
f) The Lime Walk

g) The White Garden
h) The Moat and the Orchard
i) The Tudor Buildings
j) The Herb Garden
k) The Moat Walk
l) The Tower Courtyard

A   The tower with its two octagonal turrets was completed by Sir Richard Baker shortly before Queen Elizabeth I spent three nights at Sissinghurst in August 1573. The left-hand turret contains a spiral staircase of 78 steps, while the right-hand turret forms small octagonal rooms on each of the floors above.

B   Leaving the Rondel by the south side, one comes to this delightful walk, also known as the Spring Garden. Although at other times of the year it is apt to be a little bare, in March, April and early May the two borders along each side of a flagged path, shaded by pleached limes and punctuated by garden pots from Tuscany, form a picture which reminded V. Sackville-West of the foreground of Botticelli's *Primavera*.

C   This has been described as 'the most beautiful garden at Sissinghurst, and indeed of all England.' It lies at the foot of the Priest's House, and is divided by neat low hedges of box. A path leads past the entrance of the Priest's House to a wooden door in the wall, and so back to the entrance courtyard.

D   A grass walk runs along the water's edge and at intervals small oaks and flowering trees have been planted along the top of the wall and within the orchard.

E   From the cottage garden the visitor can either walk down the brick steps on the left to the grass walk flanked on one side by a bank of azaleas and on the other by the old moat wall, or take the path through the Nuttery.

F   This garden is approached through an opening in the hedge on the left, towards the far end of the Lime Walk. Facing this gap is the South Cottage, once the end of the long south wing of the Elizabethan house.

G   The long range of buildings directly opposite the car park was built in about 1490 and the great central arch and gateway were inserted by Sir John Baker about forty years later.

H   The entrance from the tower-courtyard is by the second door on the left, coming from the front archway. From earliest times, this part of the building was the stable, and such it remained until 1930. It was dark, cold and dirty, and in transforming it into the big room we see today, the Nicholsons were obliged to insert a huge window at the north end and to build a fireplace opposite the main door, of which the chimney piece is formed by two original pieces of an Elizabethan fireplace found buried in the garden.

I   This garden depends chiefly for its effect upon old-fashioned roses, supplemented by other flowering shrubs in the long border under the wall. In the centre of the garden, formed by circular yew hedges, is the Rondel.

J   At the far end of the Nuttery, enclosed by formal yew hedges, is the little garden where grow many unusual herbs, and the paths, and even a garden seat are covered with aromatic plants.

K   From the entrance, a broad path of old London paving-stones, flanked by four great Irish yews, leads to the Elizabethan tower of three storeys, probably built about 1560–70.

L   The lawn, and the upper part of the orchard, occupy the site of the courtyard of the Elizabethan house. On the south side, by the entrance to the rose garden, is a bed of fine magnolias. The archway through the wall is known as the Bishop's Gate. On the far side of the gate is the White Garden.

(The National Trust: *Sissinghurst Castle Garden*)

Understanding text organisation

The paragraphs form a guided tour of Sissinghurst which is marked on the map.
Use the map to put the paragraphs in the order shown by the guided tour.

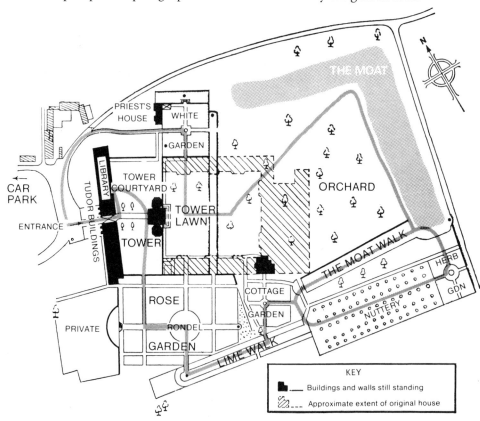

Dealing with unfamiliar words

Some of the words are the names of particular species of plants and types of trees,
or architectural features of the house. You should learn the most common words
such as *oak*, *staircase*, but for the others, you'll need to look them up in a bilingual
dictionary. Even if you don't need to know the exact meaning of a word, it's useful
to be able to recognise what family of words it belongs to. Fill in the chart below
with words from the passage.

plants/types of trees	oak
architectural features	staircase

Understanding complex sentences

1 Look at the following sentences and punctuate them. Do not look back at the text. It may help you to read them aloud.

 a) It was dark cold and dirty and in transforming it into the big room we see today the Nicholsons were obliged to insert a huge window at the north end and to build a fireplace opposite the main door of which the chimney piece is formed by two original pieces of an Elizabethan fireplace found buried in the garden.

 b) At the far end of the Nuttery enclosed by formal yew hedges is the little garden where grow many unusual herbs and the paths and even a garden seat are covered with aromatic plants.

2 Find the following sentences in the passage and answer the questions.

 a) 'The tower with its two octagonal turrets. . .' (paragraph A)
 When was the tower completed?

 b) 'Although at other times of the year. . .' (paragraph B)
 What is it that 'forms the picture'? The two borders? The flagged path? The pleached limes? The garden pots?

 c) 'A path leads past the entrance. . .' (paragraph C)
 What leads back to the entrance courtyard?

 d) 'From the cottage garden. . .' (paragraph E)
 Which way can the visitor go? Left? Right? Straight ahead?

Further work

1 Think of a house that you know well. You can choose a famous monument in your country or perhaps a friend's home. Write a guided tour of the things to see there.

2 Look through the passage and, if you've read them, the passages in units 7 and 8. Note down twenty or so of the words and expressions you have learnt. Using as much of the new vocabulary as possible write a short paragraph on one of the following subjects:

 – Describe your ideal home.
 – How to protect your home.
 – Living in a high rise block of flats.

43

Unit 10   24 hours in the life of the City

The City is a district of London in which most of the financial and commercial activities of national and international importance take place.

Reading for specific information

Look through the passage quickly and match the places in the list below with the numbers on the map.

a) Financial Times office

b) St Paul's underground station

c) Barbican Arts Centre

d) Snow Hill police station

e) Lloyds

f) Post Office

g) Sweetings fish restaurant

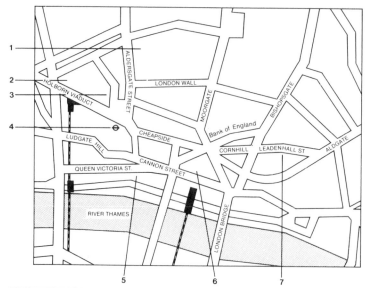

12:15 AM CHRISTINE THORN-BORROW joined the police because she wanted to work with people. Not a great deal of 5 adventure either. Like everyone else in the City police, Christine is on night shift one week out of seven and the early hours of the morning threaten to be cold. So she puts on a blue pullover under her uniform jacket before she starts out on her lonely 10 patrol from Snow Hill police station off Holborn Viaduct.

3:00 AM At the Financial Times office in Cannon Street, Ivor Barry Jones, acting night editor sits surrounded by pink and grey page proofs. Two big stories tonight. President Reagan's speech which could easily have been boring is important stuff: the US troops are pulling out of Lebanon. The other story is also important for a financial paper: the Dow Jones Index in New York has fallen sharply by 24.19 points, the biggest drop since November 1982. Jones knows there will be plenty of reaction to the fall in the morning. So he's made sure the story was covered with more accent than usual on the influences that *caused* the drop. People make big investment decisions on what they read in the FT. A false market mustn't be created.

5:25 AM The City's busiest underground station – St Paul's, in Cheapside – unlocks its gates. To get there on time the station foreman, John Milne, has to come in by bus from Goodmayes in Essex. Twenty-five minutes later, the first train arrives. Many of the passengers are post office workers and night cleaners. First at the top of the escalator is Stephen Bradley who has arrived from Upminster. He has a 6.00 am start at his office and had to get up at 4.30. As always, he got a seat and was able to sleep on the journey. A bit tiring, but then Stephen is only 18.

7:45 AM In King Edward Street, 300 yards north of St Paul's, the Post Office staff reach the climax of their morning activities. Between 7.00 and 8.00 they are working on the great bulk of letters that are to be distributed round the City during the day. Then it's on to the second delivery around midday.

9:00 AM By now the City is transformed. The tiny number of residents – 7,500, many of them caretakers, 4,000 of them living in the Barbican – is suddenly and dramatically increased. Suburban trains disgorge thousands more from suffocating carriages. Buses and Tubes add to the monstrous army of invasion which once wore top hats, changed to bowlers and these days are largely bareheaded. Furled umbrellas are now optional. Into the City's square mile are squeezed 400,000 workers. Most of them are concerned with making money.

3:00 PM Sweetings, the fish restaurant in Queen Victoria Street has served the last lunch of the day and said good-bye to the last of its 200 customers. Graham Needham, the proprietor, is already thinking of tomorrow and planning with his fishmonger, Dick Barefoot, what they should order from the coast.

4:00 PM Returning to his office from the underwriting room at Lloyds in Leadenhall Street, Bert Stratton, who specialises in accident and personal health, thinks over the risks he's been asked to cover since he drove into the City from Chigwell this morning. A varied bunch. Finally – and of all unlikely things – George Burns, the 88-year-old American comic is making some TV ads about how good smoke extractors are. An umbrella is needed because if he dies those ads could hardly be used. He chuckles, but it's a good risk; he's checked and the Burns' medical sheet shows him to be "fantastically fit".

6:00 PM The City's working day ends earlier than most of the rest of London. That's reasonable; it started earlier. By now the great exodus is nearly over.

7:00 PM The gentle strains of the harp and the flute are an overture to the night's activities at the Barbican Arts Centre, near London Wall. Later Derek Jacobi and Sinead Cusack as Benedick and Beatrice will be scratching each other's eyes out in the theatre and baritone Benjamin Luxon will be giving a Schubert recital in the concert hall. But for the moment the fort is being held by two music students.

(Janice Morley, Jane Roberts, James Hughes Onslow and Patricia Finney in *The Standard*)

Understanding text organisation

Read the passage through and then decide where the following sentences should go.

a)   Thousands pour across London Bridge.

b)   The trouble with the night patrol in the City is that there isn't anyone around.

c)   Norman Blood, 54-year-old superintendent of the post office plans to have the first delivery into every firm by 9.15.

d)   Some newspaper journalists want insurance against death or injury in Lebanon; war risks had to be high: 2½% of the indemnity for a week's cover.

Check your answers with another student.

Linking ideas

What do the words in italics refer to?

a)   '. . .there will be plenty of reaction to the *fall* in the morning.' (lines 25–6)
b)   'To get *there*. . .' (line 35)
c)   '. . .many of *them* caretakers, 4,000 of *them* living. . .' (lines 58–9)
d)   'A varied *bunch*.' (lines 87–8)
e)   '*That's* reasonable; *it* started earlier.' (lines 99–100)

Inferring

What evidence is there in the passage for the following statements?

a)   Christine Thornborrow doesn't like night shifts.
b)   *The Financial Times* takes great care how it reports the news.
c)   The bus service begins earlier than the underground.
d)   Mail is delivered more than once a day.
e)   Few people live in the City.
f)   The main events of the evening have not yet begun.

Evaluating the text

1 After reading the passage, would you describe it as: (i) factual, (ii) critical, (iii) humorous, (iv) ironic?

2 What would you say was the main aim of the author in writing the passage?

    a) To give examples of how hard people work in the City.
    b) To show how early work begins in the City.
    c) To illustrate the variety of work in the City.
    d) To draw attention to the small number of residents in the City.

Further work

1 Note down ten to twenty words or expressions from the passage and use them to write a few paragraphs about your own job, or that of someone you know well.

2 Read the passage again and note down any differences and similarities with life in your town. Think about:

    – length of working day
    – number of inhabitants
    – transport services
    – postal services
    – types of business activity
    – entertainment

Discuss with another student which aspects of life in your home town you prefer.

Unit 11   How to write a winning résumé

This passage was taken from an American magazine, and was written for women who want to return to salaried employment when they no longer need to spend so much time looking after their children.

Extracting main ideas

Read the passage and decide which *main headings* the examples below it refer to.

The main purpose of a ré-sumé is to convince an employ-er to grant you an interview.
There are two kinds. One is
5 the familiar "tombstone" that lists where you went to school and where you've worked in chronological order. The other is what I call the "functional"
10 résumé – descriptive, fun to read, unique to you and much more likely to land you an interview.

It's handy to have a "tomb-
15 stone" for certain occasions.
But prospective employers throw away most of those un-requested "tombstone" lists, preferring to interview the
20 quick rather than the dead.

What follows are tips on writing a functional résumé that will get read – a résumé that makes you come alive and
25 look interesting to employers.

Put yourself first: In order to write a résumé others will read with enthusiasm, you have to feel important about yourself.

Sell what you can do, not 30
who you are: Practice translat-ing your personality traits, character, accomplishments and achievements into skill areas. There are at least five 35 thousand skill areas in the world of work.

Toot your own horn! Many people clutch when asked to think about their abilities. 40 Some think they have none at all! But everyone does, and one of yours may just be the ticket an employer would be glad to punch – if only you 45 show it.

Be specific, be concrete, and be brief!

Turn bad news into good: Everybody has had disappoint- 50 ments in work. If you have to mention yours, look for the positive side.

Never apologize: If you're

55 returning to the work force after fifteen years as a parent, simply write a short paragraph (summary of background) in place of a chronology of experi-

60 ence. Don't apologize for working at being a mother; it's the hardest job of all. If you have no special training or higher education, just don't

65 mention education.

How to psych yourself up: The secret is to think about the *self* before you start writing about *yourself*. Take four or

70 five hours off, not necessarily consecutive, and simply write down every accomplishment in your life, on or off the job, that made you feel effective. Don't

75 worry at first about what it all means. Study the list and try to spot patterns. As you study your list, you will come closer to the meaning: identifying

80 your marketable skills. Once you discover patterns, give names to your cluster of ac- complishments (leadership skills, budget management

85 skills, child development skills etc.) Try to list at least three accomplishments under the same skills heading. Now start writing your résumé *as if you

90 mattered*. It may take four drafts or more, and several weeks, before you're ready to show it to a stranger (friends are usually too kind) for a

95 reaction. When you're satisfied, send it to a printer; a printed résumé is far superior to photo- copies. It shows an employer that you regard job hunting as

100 serious work, worth doing right.
Isn't that the kind of person you'd want working for you?

(Dick Irish in *Woman's Day*)

a) A woman who lost her job as a teacher's aide due to a cutback in government funding wrote: 'Principal of elementary school cited me as the only teacher's aide she would rehire if government funds became available.'

b) One résumé I received included the following: 'Invited by my superior to straighten out our organisation's accounts receivable. Set up orderly repayment schedule, reconciled accounts weekly, and improved cash flow 100 per cent. Rewarded with raise and promotion.'
   Notice how this woman focuses on results, specifies how she accomplished them, and mentions her reward – all in 34 words.

c) For example, if you have a flair for saving, managing and investing money, you have money management skills.

d) A woman once told me about a cash-flow crisis her employer had faced. She'd agreed to work without pay for three months until business improved. Her reward was her back pay plus a 20 per cent bonus. I asked her why that marvelous story wasn't in her résumé. She answered, 'It wasn't important.' What she was really saying of course was 'I'm not important.'

Dealing with unfamiliar words

Despite the fact that a formal style is required for writing a résumé, the author uses a fairly informal style in the article itself, and includes a number of informal or slang expressions. The alternative answers below all explain part of the word or expression in the question. But only one answer expresses its complete meaning. Choose the best answer.

a) The author calls one type of résumé a 'tombstone' (line 5) because:
    i)   it lists your achievements in chronological order.
    ii) it lists what you've done in the past rather than what you can do in the future.

b) 'Quick' (line 20) means:
    i)   fast.
    ii) efficient.
    iii) alive.

c) 'Toot your own horn!' (line 38) means:
    i)   don't be modest.
    ii) tell the employer what you've done in the past.

d) 'Many people clutch when asked to. . .' (lines 38–9) means:
    i)   many people panic.
    ii) many people underestimate themselves.

e) 'One of yours may be just the ticket an employer would be glad to punch. . .' (lines 43–5) means:
    i)   a good indication of your abilities.
    ii) something an employer might find interesting.
    iii) exactly what is required.

f) 'How to psych yourself up. . .' (line 66) means:
    i)   make a list of your abilities before you write your résumé.
    ii) how to prepare yourself mentally before writing your résumé.
    iii) what to do.

Linking ideas

Answer the following questions.

a) 'There are two kinds.' (line 4) Two kinds of what?
b) 'Everyone *does*. . .' (line 42) Everyone does what?
c) 'One of *yours*. . .' (line 43) One of your what?
d) '. . .about what *it* all means.' (lines 75–6) What does *it* mean?
e) '*It* shows an employer. . .' (line 98) What shows an employer?

Writing summaries

1 Look at the following notes made by someone preparing a résumé. Decide which points should be included in the final version.

Maybe a job as customer relations manager?
Attended Indiana University.
Left after one semester!
Studied business administration at night school.
Specialised in business application of computers.
Not sure what I'd be good at doing!
20 years raising two children.
Co-ordinated charity fund raising in town.
Invested an inheritance for 20% annual return.
Chairperson of son's school Parents-Teachers
    Association.
Sing in church choir.
Have run 5 marathons.
Helped salesman husband reorganise his filing
    system by installing a micro computer.
Worked for 3 years as secretary to the manager of
    sales division, ABC company.
Hated secretarial work!
Promoted to administrative assistant.

Get bored quickly.
Could work as administrative
    assistant.
Like flower arranging.
Look after family budget and
    save 10% of yearly income.
Like working in a team.
42 years old and only 5 years
    salaried employment!!!
Raised money for local
    church.

2 Now group the points you have chosen under the following headings.

- vocational objectives
- money management skills
- summary of background
- competitive and team skills
- management skills

3 Write the résumé for this person by joining the notes together in connected sentences under the headings above. Résumés are usually fairly concise, but you may want to use link words like *in addition, furthermore,* and *first of all, then, after this, finally.*

Further work

1 Working in pairs, discuss with your partner whether you agree with the advice given in the article. Do you think anything has been left out?
2 Write your own résumé using the techniques mentioned in the article. It doesn't matter if you're not returning to work after bringing up your children! Use at least ten words and expressions from the passage.
3 In groups of three or four, discuss whether people who have spent a long time bringing up their children should be encouraged to return to work. Compare your conclusions with another group.

Unit 12 All Greek to me

This passage is a review of the film *The Greek Tycoon*, which starred Anthony Quinn and Jacqueline Bisset. It was first released in 1978.

Extracting main ideas

Read the passage and then answer the questions.

DURING the past few months I've become increasingly fascinated by the number and variety of screen credits that appear at the beginning and, at seemingly interminable length, at the end of a film.

Often the jobs described sound exotic or strange, and frequently downright peculiar. What, for instance, is "a gaffer"? Who or what is "best boy"? What does he do? How does he justify his description? Who is he better than? I can see that there would be no credit for "worst boy", but you must admit that it's a bit puzzling.

And why is it that some films, good films too, can have less than two dozen technical credits (*Driver* with twenty-three is a good example) while other films can have over eighty?

The Greek Tycoon (*AA Plaza, Piccadilly Circus*) has eighty-three technical credits ranging from Producer to the enigmatic title "Controller". That doesn't mean that only eighty-three people were involved either, that's just categories. *The Greek Tycoon* is credited with two producers, two co-producers, three executive producers, an associate producer (notable perhaps because he's one of the few people who can be persuaded to associate with producers) *and* a production consultant. There are, in addition, credits for four Production Managers and one Production Associate. Hardly surprisingly, under the heading "Producers' Secretaries" are six names. If there are fourteen people concerned in producing one film, clearly they are going to generate a lot of paperwork, particularly if they're not speaking to each other. 40

The Greek Tycoon also excels in its music credits. They include Executive in charge of Music: David Platz. Very good too. David Platz is an experienced and successful man in the world of music and a very 45 good choice. Then there's "Music composed and orchestrated by" Stanley Myers—another top notch name. Then there's the "Main Title Theme" by John Kongos, arranged and conducted by Ron 50 Frangipane, and the credit "Music supervised and conducted by" Harry Rabinowitz, yet another excellent musician and among the top ten MD's in the world. But *then* there's a song, *Funny Kind Of Love* 55 *Affair*, sung by the delectable Madeline Bell, words and music by Mike Moran, arranged and conducted by Mike Moran. There's more. "Taverna music arranged by George Theodosiadis." The music editor is 60 Michael Clifford.

So, with music as with production, there's plenty of help around. Eight people, excluding the singer, have a hand or hands in the film's music, including, if my arith- 65 metic is kosher, three conductors. Now the ramifications of the music business have long since left me totally baffled, but that does seem rather a lot of musicians to be involved in a film that has almost no visual 70

music content with the exception of one scene in a taverna. Oh, and I forgot—there's another credit which reads "Music Recording co-ordinated by Allen
75 Steckler". I wouldn't have liked his job. All those composers to placate and having to work out who was conducting what, seeing to it that Frangipane wasn't incommoded, if that's the word, when Rabinowitz had the
80 baton, and making sure that Myers and Kongos, not to mention Moran and Theodosiadis, weren't getting invoived in demarcation disputes.

Making films like *The Greek Tycoon* is
85 tough, and if you don't believe me ask the unit publicist, or if he's on the other line the assistant unit publicist, or if she's out the assistant to the assistant unit publicist; all three are credited, as are the "Location Production Runner" ("Here's your cheese 90 and taramasalata on rye"), The Producers' Driver ("You can't *all* ride in the front"), and (and I bet he had a busy time) the Production Physician, Dr A. Chutorian.

To be fair to all concerned, the film was 95 made partly in Greece, partly in the USA and partly in Britain, and that probably explains why so many people filled so many seemingly identical roles. But to me sitting in the stalls watching the parade of names 100 go by (and subsequently checking the handout) there did seem a hell of a lot of chiefs for so few indians. The film? What was the film like? Oh, that stank.

(Barry Took in *Punch*)

In your opinion which of the following statements give an accurate summary of the passage?

a) There isn't much music in the film *The Greek Tycoon*.
b) The list of screen credits is extremely long and boring.
c) Because the film was made in three different locations, a lot of people were involved in the production.
d) There are a surprising number of people involved in making films, and a good example of this is *The Greek Tycoon*.
e) According to the critic, *The Greek Tycoon* isn't worth seeing because there are so many people involved in the production.

Linking ideas

1 What do the words in italics refer to?

    a) '. . .but you must admit that *it*'s a bit puzzling.' (lines 13–14)
    b) '("Driver" with *twenty-three* is a *good example*). . .' (lines 17–19)
    c) '*That* doesn't mean that only eighty-three. . .' (lines 23–5)
    d) '. . .but *that* does seem. . .' (lines 68–9)
    e) '. . .*all three* are credited. . .' (lines 88–9)
    f) '. . .*that* probably explains. . .' (lines 97–8)
    g) 'Oh, *that* stank!' (line 104)

2 Now answer the following questions.

    a) '. . .while other films can have over eighty?' (lines 18–19)
       Eighty what?   ⟫→

b) '. . .that's just categories.' (line 25)
   Categories of what?
c) There's more.' (line 59)
   More what?
d) '. . .involved in demarcation disputes.' (lines 82–3)
   Disputes about what?
e) '. . .a lot of chiefs for so few Indians.' (lines 102–3)
   What chiefs and Indians?

Evaluating the text

1 The writer uses humour to convey his argument, and to show how absurd the types of jobs are. Which jobs does the author find particularly strange or unnecessary? Write down the sentences in which he imagines what the jobs involve. (Note that he doesn't speculate on all of them.)

2 The article was written as a film review. What does the writer think of the film? Do you think it fair to write a review of a film like this?

Writing summaries

The following sentences are summaries of the different paragraphs in the article. There are two summaries of each paragraph. In each case, choose the best summary.

a) i) The writer has recently become interested in the number and variety of jobs involved in making films and wonders why some films have so many credits and others so few.
   ii) The writer finds the number and variety of screen credits interminable, and wonders what jobs such as 'gaffer' and 'best boy' involve.
   (paragraphs 1–3)

b) i) *The Greek Tycoon* has 83 technical credits, including Producers, Co-Producers, Executive Producers, Associate Producers, Consultant Producers, Production Managers and Secretaries.
   ii) *The Greek Tycoon* has 83 categories of technical credits including 14 producers of some kind or other.   (paragraph 4)

c) i) It also has a large number of people involved in music production, which is odd for a film which has hardly any music.
   ii) It also has a number of experienced and successful composers, singers and musicians, such as David Platz, Stanley Myers, John Kongos, Ron Frangipane, Harry Rabinowitz and Madeleine Bell.   (paragraphs 5–6)

d) i) Furthermore, making films like *The Greek Tycoon* is tough as the publicists
       will tell you; there are three of them, just in case two are busy at any time.
   ii) Furthermore, it has a number of publicists and even a production assistant.
                                                                    (paragraph 7)

e) i) The number of screen credits might be explained by the fact that it was
       filmed in three different locations, but the writer thought that there were still
       too many people. He didn't like the film either.
   ii) The film was made in Greece, USA and Britain, so this is obviously why
       there were so many people involved. But it still seemed too many chiefs for
       so few Indians.   (paragraph 8)

Further work

1 Have you ever come across an organisation where there seem to be a lot of
   workers for very little work? Discuss your experiences in groups of two or three.
   Note down any examples you can think of. Now think about your job, if you
   have one. Are you indispensable or could your work be done as efficiently by
   someone else? Ask the others in your group about their jobs.

2 Look through this passage and if you have read them, the passages in units 10
   and 11. Note down twenty or so words and expressions which you have learnt.
      Using as much of the new vocabulary as possible, write a paragraph on one of
   the following subjects:

   – Describe a day in your working life (or that of someone you know well).
   – Job sharing – the solution to unemployment?
   – What are the advantages and disadvantages of working in the town as
     opposed to the countryside?

Unit 13   Shopping basket psychology

Predicting

1 Look at the title of the unit. Discuss with another student what you think it means.
2 Now write down 10–15 words which you expect to see in the passage. Can you predict what the passage is likely to say?
3 As you read the passage, answer the questions. Try not to look at the rest of the passage.

I FELT hostility flowing from the woman standing behind me in the supermarket check-out line. She rocked back and forth on her heels impatiently
5 and drummed on her handbag.

Had I cut in front of her? Her eyes wouldn't meet mine. She was glaring into my basket. I quickly surveyed my selections to see what could be generating such hostility. 10

Let's see: two bottles of champagne, a chunk of Roquefort, a lovely avocado, a bottle of capers, three limes, a pound of shrimp, and a quart of Perrier water. 15

a) What kind of life style do you think the writer has? What kind of home does she have?

It was a mixed bag to be sure. However, as I am a working widow with an empty nest, I am no longer a slave to menus planned for the masses.
20 Five years ago I enjoyed cooking for a six-foot four-inch husband, teen-aged sons, and their starving friends. Today I adore the luxury of eating what and when I choose.

Still looking for the answer to the 25 woman's puzzling behavior, I looked down into her cart and shuddered: Three gallons of milk; six loaves of bread; ten pounds of hamburger; four chickens; a mountain of baby-food 30 jars; two racks of soft drinks; ice cream, cakes, and pies.

b) What kind of life style does this woman have? Where does she live? Who lives with her?

Studying the contents of her basket, I could easily visualize her life style
35 and all the hard work that goes into raising a young family. Obviously, she could sense my self-indulgent style too.

Since that encounter, I have become more aware of what a grocery list 40 reveals. If body language can tell a stranger a lot about one's personality, so can the fruits of your shopping expedition.

45   For example, yesterday I stood behind an individual who obviously was not into being the perfect housewife. While her little boy begged unsuccessfully for a cookie, she unpacked shampoo, hair conditioner, fingernail-polish 50 remover, cotton balls, two movie magazines, and five pounds of cat litter. I could see her starving family facing the bare pantry. There wasn't even any food for the cat.   55

c) So what do these shopping items tell you about the person who is buying them?

I especially like to observe male shoppers. I don't mean the docile chaps dutifully checking items off a list. I prefer the gourmet who knows what he wants: imported cheeses, exotic 60 spices, a whole leg of lamb, early asparagus, or artichokes.

d) What is this shopper's life style likely to be?

It doesn't take much imagination to place him in a smartly decorated bach-65 elor pad making a splendid repast for friends.
   Many of the young wives are terrific shoppers too. Last week I trailed a fresh-looking girl in blue jeans with two children. She chose fresh fruits and 70 vegetables with admirable judgment and carefully selected the ingredients for a beef stew, lasagne, and perhaps coq au vin.

e) What about this woman's life style? Can you imagine her home?

75 Mentally I placed her in a modest but charming cottage, cooking appetizing healthy meals for her family. Lucky husband, lucky children. Another interesting type is the Eskimo whose every choice is frozen. 80 Frozen *guacamole* dip, frozen pancake mix, frozen *enchiladas*.

f) What about this person's home? What does it look like?

I think of this person at home in a high-tech apartment, punching in the micro-85 wave code to defrost frozen lettuce, frozen peanut butter, and frozen Jello.
   The next time you are stuck behind someone, try my little game: Look at the cart ahead of you. Are there 90 children in the household? Pets? Someone who is dieting? Someone who isn't but probably should be? Do they shop once a month, loading three carts, or every day, racing through the express lane? Is the emphasis on fresh 55 or canned? Would you want to be joining them for dinner tonight? What do you suppose the kitchen looks like? Before you know it, you will hear those heavenly words, "Next please".   100

(Gloria Morris, reprinted by permission of *American Way*, inflight magazine of American Airlines, copyright 1983 by American Airlines.)

4   Check whether the words you predicted in 2 appeared in the passage. If they didn't, discuss with your partner whether they might have.

Extracting main ideas

Look through the passage again and then decide which of the following sentences best expresses its main point.

a) 'Today I adore the luxury of eating what and when I choose.'
b) 'Studying the contents of her basket, I could easily visualize her life style and all the hard work that goes into raising a young family.'
c) 'If body language can tell a stranger a lot about one's personality, so can the fruits of your shopping expedition.'
d) 'I especially like to observe male shoppers.'
e) 'The next time you are stuck behind someone, try my little game.'

Understanding text organisation

There are a number of adverbs in the passage. There are two types:

Type A refers to what the writer is describing or how something is being done.
   Example: 'I *quickly* surveyed my selections. . .' (lines 8–9)
Type B refers to the writer's own point of view and signals his or her reaction to what is being described.
   Example: '*Obviously*, she could sense my self-indulgent style. . .' (lines 36–7)

Decide whether the following words in italics are type A or type B adverbs.

a) '. . .to place him in a *smartly* decorated bachelor pad. . .' (lines 64–5)
b) '*Mentally* I placed her in a modest but charming cottage. . .' (lines 75–6)
c) 'She rocked back and forth on her heels *impatiently*. . .' (lines 3–4)
d) 'I *especially* like to observe male shoppers.' (lines 56–7)
e) '. . .I stood behind an individual who *obviously* was not into. . .' (lines 45–7)
f) While her little boy begged *unsuccessfully* for a cookie. . .' (lines 48–9)

Linking ideas

To avoid repeating themselves, writers sometimes refer to *one* idea in a variety of different ways. This passage explains how to analyse people's life styles by looking at the *contents of their shopping basket*. What other words and expressions are used to refer to the contents of the shopping basket?
Example: 'grocery list' (line 40)

Writing summaries

1 The passage is organised in the following way:

exposition In this section the writer sets the scene, preparing the reader for the main point. (lines 1–36)

main point This section explains what the writer is writing about. (lines 39–44)

example(s) These help to illustrate the main point. (lines 45–86)

conclusion In this passage, the conclusion makes a direct appeal to the reader by suggesting that he/she should try out the writer's theory the next time he/she is in a supermarket. (lines 87–100)

Answer the following questions in note form.
a) In the exposition, what was generating the woman's hostility? What was the writer's reaction to the contents of the woman's basket?
b) According to the writer, what does a grocery list reveal?
c) What are the four examples that the writer gives of her theory?
d) What does the writer suggest you do the next time you're in a supermarket?

2 Now make sentences from your notes. Make sure you include all the necessary information. Join the sentences together into a paragraph summarising the passage.

3 When you have finished, re-read the passage and make sure there is nothing important you have left out.

Further work

1 Make a list of the things you buy when you go to the supermarket. Use as many words and expressions from the passage as possible. Hand it to another student who you don't know very well, and look at his/her list. Try and think of what his or her life style is like. Write a few lines describing it. Now find other people in the class who have lists which are similar to your partner's. Are the descriptions of the life styles similar too?

2 Re-read the last paragraph and then, working in pairs, think of other games you can play in your head to make the time pass when you are waiting in a queue.

Inferring

Read the passage and then decide what evidence there is in the text for the statements which are printed below it. If there is no evidence, or the statements are false, explain what the passage really says.

The Case of the Broken Chair
The first in a new series of true stories
by the intrepid septuagenarian **EDWARD HORNBY**

SOME time ago I discovered that one of the chairs in my front hall had a broken leg. I didn't foresee any great difficulty in getting it mended, as there are a whole lot of antique shops in the Pimlico Road which is three minutes' walk from my flat, so I set forth one morning carrying the chair with me. I went into the first shop confidently expecting a friendly reception, with a kindly man saying, 'What a charming chair, yes that's quite a simple job, when would you want it back?'

I was quite wrong. The man I approached wouldn't look at it. I wasn't too concerned; after all, it was only the first try and there are many more shops on both sides of the road.

The reaction at the second shop, though slightly politer, was just the same, and at the third and the fourth – so I decided that my approach must be wrong.

I entered the fifth shop with some confidence because I had concocted a plan. I placed the chair gently on the floor so as not to disturb the damaged leg and said 'Would you like to buy a chair?' The rather fierce proprietor looked it over carefully and said, 'Yes, not a bad little chair, how much do you want for it?' '£20,' I said. 'OK,' he said, 'I'll give you £20.' 'It's got a slightly broken leg,' I said. 'Yes, I saw that, it's nothing, don't worry about it.'

Everything was going to plan and I was getting excited. 'What will you do with it?' I asked. 'Oh, it will be very saleable once the repair is done, I like the bit of old green velvet on the top, I shall leave that, yes, very saleable.' 'I'll buy it,' I said. 'What d'ye mean? You've just sold it to me,' he said. 'Yes I know but I've changed my mind; as a matter of fact it is just what I'm looking for – I've got a pair to it at home, I'll give you 27 quid for it.' 'You must be crazy,' he said; then suddenly the penny dropped and he smiled and said, 'I know what you want, you want me to mend your chair.' 'You're plumb right,' I said.

'And what would you have done if I had walked in and said "Would you mend this chair for me?"' 'I wouldn't have done it,' he said, 'We don't do repairs, not enough money in it and too much of a nuisance, but I'll mend this for you, shall we say a fiver?' He was a very nice man and thought the whole episode rather funny.

(*The Observer*)

a) Mr Hornby carried the broken chair to Pimlico Road because he didn't have a car.

Example: a) No evidence; all we know is that Pimlico Road isn't very far from the writer's flat.

b) Many antique shops often do furniture repairs.
c) Mr Hornby felt that the first shop proprietor was rather rude.
d) He decided that he had approached the shops in the wrong order.
e) In the fifth shop, he tried at first to disguise the fact that the chair was broken.
f) The proprietor thought he could sell the chair for more than £20.
g) Once he was in the shop, Mr Hornby suddenly decided not to sell the chair.
h) The man only offered to mend the chair because he was amused by Mr Hornby's approach.

Dealing with unfamiliar words

Choose the best answer for the words in italics.

a) 'I *set forth* one morning. . .' (line 11): This is likely to mean (i) left home, (ii) made plans, (iii) made it known.
b) '. . .*after all*, it was only. . .' (lines 20–1): Here, this means (i) despite, (ii) nevertheless, (iii) because.
c) '. . .I had *concocted* a plan.' (lines 30–1): This probably means (i) thought of, (ii) forgotten, (iii) changed.
d) 'Everything was *going to plan*. . .' (line 42): This means that the plan was (i) not successful, (ii) impractical, (iii) working as intended.
e) '. . .the bit of old green *velvet*. . .' (line 46): This is a kind of (i) wood, (ii) cloth, (iii) metal.
f) 'I've got *a pair to it*. . .' (lines 52–3): This means that he's got (i) two more chairs like it, (ii) one more chair like it at home.
g) '. . .then suddenly the *penny dropped*. . .' (lines 55–6): This means (i) the proprietor understood Mr Hornby's plan, (ii) the proprietor changed his mind, (iii) the proprietor accepted some money.   ⋙→

h) 'You're *plumb right.* . .' (lines 58–9): This probably means (i) almost right, (ii) quite right, (iii) quite wrong.

i) '. . .*too much of a nuisance.* . .' (line 65): This means (i) repairs cause too much trouble, (ii) Mr Hornby's chair is too badly damaged, (iii) the repair will cause Mr Hornby too much trouble.

Understanding text organisation

Sometimes discourse markers are left out because the context clearly shows how the parts of a sentence are related to each other. Insert *because, but* or *so* in suitable places in the sentences below.

a) 'Yes, I saw that, it's nothing. . .' (line 40)
b) 'I like the bit of old green velvet on the top, I shall leave that. . .' (lines 46–7)
c) 'It is just what I'm looking for. . . I'll give you 27 quid for it.' (lines 53–4)
d) 'We don't do repairs, (there's) not enough money in it. . .' (lines 63–4)

Writing summaries

Use the passage to put the following sentences in the order of events described in the passage. Then link the sentences together using the following words: *however, so, and, then, but*. You can use either the same number of sentences or fewer, but make sure you punctuate them correctly.

a) The proprietor suddenly realised Mr Hornby wanted to have the chair mended rather than sell it.
b) In the fifth shop he tried selling the chair rather than asking for it to be mended.
c) Mr Hornby had a chair with a broken leg.
d) Amused by the whole episode, he agreed to mend it for £5.
e) When the proprietor agreed to buy it and had explained what he would do with it, Mr Hornby offered to buy it back.
f) To his surprise, none of the first four shops he tried were prepared to do the repair.
g) He didn't expect any difficulty in getting it mended.

Evaluating the text

1 Mr Hornby is described as 'the intrepid septuagenarian', which means that he is brave and over 70 years old. Why do you think he's described in this way?

2 Which of the following words would you use to describe:

   a) Mr Hornby?
   b) the proprietors in the first four shops?
   c) the proprietor of the fifth shop?

   obstinate   ingenious   unhelpful   good-humoured

Further work

Work in groups of two or three. Discuss what services and facilities have changed since you were a child.

   Make a list of the changes, noting which are for the better and which are for the worse. Think about aspects such as:

— public transport
— the expected life of consumer products
— shopping facilities
— work and leisure activities
— media services

Compare your list with another group. Choose three positive changes and three negative ones. Then discuss with other groups which are the most important changes to have occurred in your lifetime.

Unit 15 Commercial break

Extracting main ideas

The advertisement opposite is for Irish whis*key*, which is made in a similar way to Scotch whis*ky*, but is not as well-known.

Read the passage and then decide which of the following sentences would be the best slogan:

- Ice-cold Scotch on a hot summer's day.
- Irish or Scotch. Which is more romantic?
- The taste of Ireland.
- As smooth as a spring in summer.
- In pursuit of good taste.

Inferring

Answer the following questions.

a) Would you say that Jameson's was a well-known brand of whiskey?
b) 'It was love at first sight.' What is the writer referring to?
c) How old do you think the writer is?
d) Do you think the writer trusted the woman's opinion of Jameson's?
e) What does 'excellent taste' refer to?

It was love at first sight, I suppose. And yet it wasn't just the way she looked. It was also the way she talked.

We'd been for a stroll in the country, one lazy, hazy summer Saturday. I felt about sixteen again–walking close enough for our hands to keep touching, in the hope that she might hang on.

At a little country pub overlooking Evesham Vale, I popped the inevitable question.

"I'll have a Jameson," she replied.

"A what?"

"A Jameson. You know, the famous Irish whiskey."

"Oh," I said somewhat blankly.

"Haven't you tried it?" She said, laughing. "Don't look so amazed, it's great. Made from the finest Irish barley, the softest spring water, and it's distilled three times, so it's really smooth."

"Two Jameson, please," I said to the barman a moment later. And before rejoining my partner I took a little sip–just to see if she was right.

"Was I right?" She said. "I saw you taking a crafty swig!"

"Excellent taste," I said.

She raised an eyebrow quizzically. "Are you talking about me, or the Jameson?"

You'll never know until you've tried it.

65

Extracting main ideas

Look at the advertisement opposite and decide what its main idea is. Choose from the list below.

a) Crest Hotels do their best to make their guests feel at home.
b) Crest Hotels mostly cater for businessmen/women.
c) The guests in Crest Hotels will find all the facilities they require in the building itself.
d) Crest Hotels take great care in looking after businesswomen as well as businessmen.

Inferring

What evidence is there in the passage for the following statements?

a) Businesswomen in hotel restaurants are usually seated at the worst tables.
b) Women in bars are usually regarded as being there to pick men up.
c) Other hotels are decorated in brighter colours.
d) Crest Hotels provide equipment which is usually too bulky to carry in your luggage.
e) Crest Hotels are not patronising towards women guests.

What I'm really trying to say is that they treat me like a person.

A rather over-used phrase, I agree, but other businesswomen will know what I mean.

If I'm in the restaurant, there's none of that over-effusive welcome, followed by a table behind a pillar or near the kitchen door.

"I've finally found a hotel that treats me like a man."

I don't have to take my briefcase into the bar either, to prove all I want is a drink.

When I go to my room, there are some little extra touches that make me feel especially welcome.

It's not simply the softer decor. Crest have thoughtfully provided a hairdryer and make-up mirror, things I appreciate away from home.

And they can even come up with an iron or a pair of tights at a moment's notice.

So I always stay at a Crest Hotel whenever I can. I like their friendly and businesslike attitude towards me.

And speaking as a woman, you can't say fairer than that.

Crest Hotels International

Nobody works harder to make your stay better.

Extracting main ideas

Look at the following advertisement and decide what its main idea is. Choose from the list below.

a) It stresses the uncertainty and critical nature of the international situation in order to recruit officers into the army.
b) It suggests that despite the mixture of boredom and danger, life as an officer is extremely enjoyable.
c) It suggests that the Army will allow you to travel the world and meet people.
d) It appeals to the patriotism of the reader to join the Army and defend his country and the free world.

Will Russian tanks roar across the plains of Germany?

Will crises erupt somewhere so remote we all have to
5 scour maps to find out where it is?

Will one of our NATO allies call for moral support on its borders?

10 Will we be asked to join an international peace-keeping force to separate the sides in a civil war?

Frankly, your guess is as
15 good as ours.

The world is so unstable it could go critical at any time without so much as a warning light.

20 This is why we have made the Army much more mobile.

And why we always try to recruit the type of young man who can add calmness and
25 good humour to a tense situation.

Now we need another 900 young Officers whom these men will follow, if necessary,
30 to the ends of the earth.

A job with no guarantee of success.

You may well argue that your joining the Army would not have saved one life in
35 Afghanistan.

We would go further, it might not save anyone's life, including your own.

On the other hand, it
40 might.

It might, if enough like-minded men join with you, help to prevent a nuclear war.

And it might, just might,
45 hold the world together long enough for the powers of freedom and sweet reasonableness to prevail.

Some hopes?
50 Perhaps. But the alternative is no hope at all.

Hoping for the best, preparing for the worst.

55 Your part in this will be to prepare for a war everyone

prays will never happen.

Depending on the job you choose, you will rehearse battle tactics in Germany.

Confront heat in Cyprus, Belize or Hong Kong.

And heat of a different sort in Northern Ireland.

You will practise, repair, train and try to forge links with your men that will withstand fire.

Occasionally, you may be asked to clamber into a VC10 on the way to, well, somewhere like monitoring a cease-fire in Rhodesia.

But more often, the worst enemy your men will face will be boredom, when it will take all your skills as a teacher and manager to motivate them.

Then it will be difficult to remember that you are still protecting your country and all you love most.

An easy question to dodge.

The question is, are you prepared to take the job on for three years or longer?

No one will accuse you if you don't.

Women won't send you white feathers and children won't ask what you did in the war.

All we ask is that every young man at least takes the question seriously and answers it to the satisfaction of his own conscience.

This way we are bound to get our 900 new Officers.

If you are undecided but want to take the matter a stage further without committing yourself in any way, write to Major John Floyd, Army Officer Entry, Department A12, Lansdowne House, Berkeley Square, London W1X 6AA.

Tell him your date of birth, your educational qualifications and why you want to join us.

He will send you booklets to give you a far larger picture of the life and, if you like, put you in touch with people who can tell you more about the career.

 **Army Officer**

Evaluating the text

With another student, look back at all three advertisements and answer the following question.

The intention of most advertisements is to persuade the reader in some way, but the style may have other intentions as well. Decide what intentions the advertisements in this unit have. Choose from the list below.

a) to inform　　　　f) to amuse
b) to entertain　　　g) to criticise
c) to provoke　　　　h) to shock
d) to teach　　　　　i) to predict the future
e) to threaten　　　　j) to reassure

Justify your answers to your partner.

Reacting to the text

1 The following letter was written to the newspaper which published one of the advertisements. Which advertisement do you think the letter is referring to? Discuss with your partner whether you think the criticism is justified.

> Sir,—I hope this letter is one of an avalanche sent to you to complain about the advertisement for..........I find the psychological blackmail—so ineptly expressed especially in the last section　—　ludicrous　and dangerous.
> Yours sincerely,
> . . .

2 Think about the intention of each advertisement. Which advertisements would you expect to be successful? Discuss your views with another student.

Further work

1 Work in groups of two or three. Make a list of all the places where you find advertising. Think about TV, radio, cinema as well as bags, signs and posters. Choose two of the most effective types of advertising. Then look for examples of these types of advertising. Prepare a short presentation for the rest of the class with your ideas on effective advertising. When everyone is ready, give your presentation to the class.

2 Look through the passages in this unit and, if you have read them, the passages in units 13 and 14. Note down twenty or so words and expressions which you have learnt. Using as much of the new vocabulary as possible, write a short paragraph on one of the following subjects:

   - Describe and discuss one of your favourite advertisements.
   - The advantages and disadvantages of supermarket shopping.
   - What makes advertising effective?

Unit 16   This way for suite dreams

Predicting

1 This passage describes the features that its writer expects to find in his 'Dream Hotel'. It also includes the features which might be found in a 'Nightmare Hotel'. Before you read the passage, decide which of the following words you would expect to find in the passage, and in what sort of context. If you don't understand all the words, check their meaning in a dictionary.

steroid	beverage
shove	de luxe
reception	servant
nervous breakdown	fire escape
patronise	room service
laundry	lift

2 Now read the passage and check whether the words you chose in 1 appeared or not. Which words might have appeared but didn't?

One of the factors that sets Dream Hotels apart is the speed and willingness with which the staff do their jobs. Take room service. In your really classy Dream Hotel this function is performed by an élite corps of deaf
10 mutes who, especially when they're bringing breakfast, know that you do not wish to speak. They maintain a monastic silence in your presence. They bring you food that is hot.
15 They accept your tip, even if it's in the wrong currency, with a small reverential bow. Then, pocketing your worthless dong or piastre without a murmur, they depart as
20 quickly and quietly as they came.

Compare that with the kind of thing one is likely to find in the lesser British hostelries patronised by us working journos. When you ring for room service the man at the desk 25 often doesn't know what room service is. You urge him to make a few inquiries, and eventually, sucking hard at his teeth, he connects you to the laundry. When you finally get 30 through to the appropriate person, you ask, let us say, for tea and toasted sandwiches. Then you must be patient. During the time it takes to come you can write a novel, go 35 bald, change sex, perhaps even retire. And when it does arrive, of course, it isn't toasted sandwiches at all. It's yesterday's scones. And the pot contains tepid water and a solitary tea- 40 bag floating on the surface like a dead frog in a pond.

The kind of personal service I'm talking about is best exemplified by a

72

45 certain type of South Korean geisha house where the guest, from the moment he enters the door, *does not use his hands*. His jacket is removed by a sylph who then sits him down,
50 removes his tie, lifts the glass to his lips, knots a napkin around his neck and proceeds to shove dinner into his mouth. Afterwards she wipes the gravy from his chin, scratches his
55 ear, loosens his belt, tips the cognac down his throat and, from time to time, slides a smouldering Romeo y Julieta between his teeth.

You may find that kind of atten-
60 tion somewhat excessive. If so, how else do you judge a Dream Hotel? Well, a significant indicator of the standards it aspires to is its lifts. Though they may be driven by men
65 dressed like Mexican generals, the machines themselves seem to have borrowed various important design details from the people who invented the padded cell. A real five-star de
70 luxe lift *ought* to have a small, well-stocked bar in the corner, together with a gypsy violinist and a waiter ready to offer the traveller a glass of gin and an onion on a stick whenever
75 he steps aboard. The potential of the lift as a social centre, a place for businessmen or lovers to meet, has not yet, alas, been recognised by even the most enlightened managements.
80 The worst hotel lifts in the world – and, for that matter, the worst hotels – are in Russia. Several years ago I had the misfortune to stay at a Moscow establishment so dreadful
85 that its name, mercifully, has been utterly erased from my memory. But it was about 80 storeys high, and built by Stalin when his megalomania was starting to give his
90 doctors serious cause for concern. My room was just under the roof and, when the view wasn't locked in by 10/10ths cloud cover, I was able to nod to the Aeroflot pilots engaged

in a holding pattern over the city. 95 My only way back to earth, other than through the window, was by the lifts. These were operated by female hammer-throwers disqualified from competition because they'd overdone 100 the steroids and their chests were getting hairy. A 15-minute wait for a lift was routine. But then, having opened her doors, the operator liked to pretend she hadn't seen you and, 105 playfully, crashed them shut again in your face.

I got around that one by using the Lipstick Tactic. Advised by a friend who had stayed there before, I 110 entered the USSR with several dozen of the things. 'As soon as you get to the hotel, start passing them about,' she said. 'Word will spread. Favours will be granted.' Well, she was right. 115 The lipsticks got me lift rides, and the lipsticks got me food. I now realise, in retrospect, that the function of the waitresses down in the vast, echoing restaurant was to hold 120 up the pillars. The provision of meals or service was not listed among their duties. For hour after hour they leant heroically against their concrete columns, clearly aware that 125 even a few seconds' absence would pose grave threats to the structural integrity of the building.

But I got my dinner, and I got it fast, by standing a 130 Boots's 17 Gleamer in 'Satsuma' between my knife and fork the instant I sat down. Others were not so lucky. One evening I 135 shared my table with an Arab who, faint with hunger, eventually laid his head on the placemat and began weeping. I found myself witnessing a full-scale nervous breakdown, but 140 though it distressed me, it didn't distress the waitresses. Grins flickered from pillar to pillar. They thought it was good cabaret.

(Alexander Frater in *The Observer Colour Magazine*)

Extracting main ideas

1 Decide whether each paragraph refers to the writer's 'Dream Hotel' or his 'Nightmare Hotel'.
2 Now fill in the chart below with information from the passage. Not all the boxes can be filled in.

	Dream hotel	*Nightmare hotel*
hotel service		
food		
lifts		
restaurant service		

Dealing with unfamiliar words

1 Choose the best answer.

   a) 'classy' (line 7): Is a classy hotel likely to be (i) a very good one, (ii) a very bad one?
   b) 'élite' (line 9): Is an élite corps of servants likely to be (i) very ordinary, (ii) very special?
   c) 'enlightened' (line 79): This is (i) a positive or (ii) a negative quality.
   d) 'megalomania' (line 89): This is likely to be something which affected Stalin's (i) finances, (ii) policies.

2 Even some native speakers of English might find some of the following words difficult, and would have to look at the context to understand them. Look at the words from the passage on the left and match them with their probable meanings on the right.

   a) 'dong/piastre' (line 18)   i)   journalists
   b) 'hostelries' (line 23)   ii) slim, graceful woman
   c) 'journos' (line 24)   iii) foreign coin
   d) 'sylph' (line 49)   iv) heavyweight athletes
   e) 'hammer-throwers' (line 99)   v)   lipstick
   f) 'Boot's 17 Gleamer in "Satsuma"' (lines 131–2)   vi) hotels

Understanding writer's style

1 The writer gives several humorous and exaggerated descriptions of hotel service which he is either praising or criticising.

For example: 'For hour after hour they leant heroically against their concrete columns, clearly aware that even a few seconds' absence would pose grave threats to the structural integrity of the building.' (lines 123–8)

Here the writer is humorously describing why it might be that the waitresses are leaning against the columns. But in fact he is criticising the poor service in the restaurant.

Find other humorous and exaggerated descriptions in the passage and discuss with another student whether the writer is praising or criticising.

2 Choose the best answer.

a) The writer says 'This function is performed by an élite corps of deaf mutes' (lines 8–10)
   i) to give a humorous example of the kind of discreet service he requires.
   ii) to suggest that the best hotel staff are not very communicative.

b) 'During the time it takes to come. . .' (lines 34–6) suggests that:
   i) there's plenty to do in British hotels.
   ii) the service is extremely slow.

c) 'Afterwards she wipes the gravy from his chin. . .' (lines 54–8)
   i) gives further examples of personal service in Dream Hotels.
   ii) suggests that the guest is usually uncomfortable after being fed.

d) 'These were operated by female hammer-throwers. . .' (lines 98–102) suggests that:
   i) the faulty lifts were driven more by physical strength than by mechanical means.
   ii) the female lift attendants were not very attractive.

Further work

1 Work in groups of two or three. Look at the passage in this unit again and decide which of the features described you would like to see in your idea of a dream hotel. Think about what you would like to do there, the service, facilities etc. When you have all agreed on your idea of a dream hotel, write a short paragraph describing it.

2 Write a paragraph describing a stay in either a very good or a very bad hotel. Use at least ten words and expressions from this passage.

Unit 17 Clearing customs

Reading for specific information

The following passage gives advice on customs and protocol in a variety of
different countries. Read the letters below which ask for specific advice and then
look at the passage to see if you can find information to answer them. Don't spend
more than three minutes on this exercise.

I'm the overseas representative for a firm which manufactures cosmetics
and perfumes. I'm going to France and Spain to see if I can introduce
my company's products into these markets. Do you have any advice for
businessmen and women visiting these countries?

My husband's firm has suggested that I accompany him on a tour of Korea,
China and Japan next autumn. I'm told that wives are not usually invited
to take part in the many social activities which a business trip like
this usually involves. Is this true? I don't want to spend my time
sitting in a hotel room. And if I do go, what advice do you have about
protocol for both me and my husband?

I've heard that the formalities involved in business dealings in the
Middle East are rather complex. Can you give me any tips as I'm off
to the Gulf States on a business trip next month?

Gestures aren't the only area in which the unwary traveler can get tripped up. Foreign cultures adhere to different business customs and protocol. For example:

5 • Caffeine junkies should restrain themselves in the Middle East. "Three cups of tea or coffee is usually the polite limit in offices and during social calls," counsels "Travel Pak," a free publication of Alia, the
10 Royal Jordanian Airline. "But if your host keeps going, you also may continue sipping. If you've had your fill, give your empty cup a quick twist – a sort of wiggle – as you hand it back. That means, 'No
15 more, thank you.'"

• Middle East visitors also should not be surprised "if others barge right into the office in the middle of your conversation with the person you are seeing," notes "Travel Pak." An old Arab custom calls 20 for keeping an "open office."

• The British, however, consider it impolite to interrupt a visitor, even after all business has been transacted. The commercial caller is expected to be sensitive 25 to this point, know when to stop, and initiate his or her own departure.

• Spanish businesspeople "connect" with tangibles, advises Karen Weiner Escalera, president of a New York City 30 public-relations company. She notes that samples of products or services should be offered whenever possible. And, she points out, in Spain "offices and retail establish-

35 ments generally close from 1:00 p.m. to as late as 4:30 p.m." Her husband, Alfonso Escalera, U.S. representative for the Spanish Line shipping company, adds that black shoes, not brown, are con-
40 sidered proper for business occasions. The Spanish historically have favored black and ultradark colors.

• Good office manners in Indonesia require the visitor to present a business card
45 immediately. If no card is offered, long delays may result. The mark of a thoughtful executive is to have one side in English and the other in Bahasa. In Japan a visitor should be prepared to distribute as many
50 as 40 business cards a day. Protocol in France calls for listing academic credentials on one's calling cards.

• In Japan certain guests at evening business gatherings will leave early. They
55 should be allowed to leave without effusive good-bys. The Japanese consider formal departures to be disruptive in such cases and disturbing to remaining guests.

• In Scandinavia and Finland business
60 guests may be asked to shed their clothes and join their hosts in a sauna. The invitation is a sign that a good working relationship has been established.

• In Denmark a visitor who is invited to a
65 business associate's home should take flowers or some unusual delicacy.

• In Norway, to be totally correct, the visitor should send a gift the day after the dinner.
70 • In France always send flowers before visiting a home for dinner. But don't send chrysanthemums; they're for funerals. (More than flowers and gifts, the French prefer a business visitor to sponsor a
75 special occasion after major dealings.)

• In West Germany flowers are an appropriate gift to take to a business colleague's wife when invited to dinner. But don't bring red roses; they're for lovers.
80 • In Switzerland red roses are OK as long as they don't number 3. "Take 1 or take 20, but 3 signifies you're sweet-

hearts," explains Erika Faisst of the Swiss National Tourist Office.

• Young Korean businessmen expect 85 their wives to be invited by foreigners to attend business or pleasure meetings in the evening. They also expect their wives to decline the invitation.

• In Korea guests of honor (as well as the 90 elderly and revered) are supposed to serve themselves first from community dishes. Good manners, however, require that the foreign guest of honor decline the privilege at least once, sometimes twice. 95

• In Mexico hands should be kept on the table during meals.

• In the Arab world, the word *no* must be mentioned three times before it is accepted. In contrast, it is considered good 100 business manners to make many and long efforts to pick up the check.

• In Spain "psst, psst" is an acceptable way to call a waiter; in India whistling is considered offensive. 105

• In Germany men are expected to stand when a woman rises from the table and when she returns. Fortunately, German women have reached a silent understanding that when one has to be excused, all 110 take advantage of the opportunity.

• In the People's Republic of China, gift giving is considered an insult, says Patrick J. Lewis, president of Club Universe, a Los Angeles tour operator. "If you want to give 115 someone a gift, make sure it's modest in value. This will not be considered offensive, but it may be declined." The Chinese manner of expressing friendship and welcome is to clap, Lewis adds. "You may be 120 greeted with clapping when entering a factory, hospital, commune, or school. Politeness dictates that you respond with applause, even though it may seem like you're clapping for yourself." 125

• In Singapore and the Soviet Union, locals are uncomfortable around men with long hair or beards. Public places in Singapore post signs reading, "Males with long hair will be attended to last." 130

(Bill Hunter, reprinted by permission of *American Way*, inflight magazine of American Airlines, copyright 1983 by American Airlines)

Reacting to the text

1 Work in groups of two or three. Do you know any of the countries mentioned in
the passage? Does it mention the customs in your country? If so, do you agree or
disagree with the advice given? If not, tell the other students what you should do
in social or business situations in your country. If they are from the same
country, do they agree with you?

2 What other social customs and examples of business protocol have you noticed
in any of the foreign countries you have visited? Tell the others about them.

Inferring

Read the passage again. With another student, discuss what evidence there is for
the following statements. If there is no evidence, explain what the passage really
says.

a) In the Middle East, it is customary to drink three cups of coffee.
b) Uninvited visitors are welcome in Middle Eastern offices.
c) In Britain, business visitors can stay as long as they like.
d) The best time to visit offices in Spain is in the morning or late afternoon.
e) If you leave a business meeting in Japan early, do so discreetly.
f) Don't bother to take a swimming costume to Scandinavia.
g) In certain countries, it's better to avoid giving red roses as a present.
h) Wives of Korean businessmen do not usually attend social occasions.
i) In the Middle East, the guest always pays the bill.
j) It is not customary to give gifts in China.

Writing summaries

1 Look through the passage again and complete the table below. Some of it has already been done for you.

	business protocol	social customs	gifts	clothing/ appearance	eating/ drinking
Middle East					Considered impolite to drink more than 3 cups of coffee unless your host drinks more.
Britain					
Spain					
Indonesia	Business cards in 2 languages. Present them immediately.				
Japan					
France					
Scandinavia		You may be invited to join your hosts in a sauna.			
West Germany					
Switzerland					
Korea					
Mexico					
China					
Singapore					
Soviet Union					

2 Write short answers to the letters on page 76.

Further work

1 How important do you think it is to respect the protocol and customs when you are in foreign countries? Tell your partner about any embarrassing experiences you have had, or have heard about. Visit other pairs and tell each other about your experiences.
2 Write a short paragraph about social customs and business protocol in your country. Use at least ten words and expressions from the passage in this unit.

Unit 18 Getting China cracked

Extracting main ideas

This passage was written by an English journalist and consists of a number of questions and answers about visiting China for the first time. However, the questions do not match the answers. Work with another student and read the passage through. Then match the questions with their corresponding answers.

1 **Is it easy to get about?**

A If you are with a party, your guide will know what to do. But you can go out on your own: China is a very safe place to wander about in (although crossing roads has its dangers) and the Chinese are hospitable and helpful to foreigners. If you get lost you are likely to be escorted back to the hotel (take a card with the name of the hotel on it if you have a poor sense of direction).

2 **Are there many places to stay?**

B Billions. Guidebooks give the addresses of major restaurants and you can ask your guide to arrange a meal in them (at between 15 and 60 yuan per head): but you should also eat in an ordinary restaurant. The Chinese eat early, lunching at 11.30am to 12 noon, dining from 5pm. By 7pm the floor will be being washed around your feet. You will have to search for a place to sit among a crowd of diners, and the menu will be chalked up on a blackboard in Chinese characters; but as the names of the dishes are not strictly descriptive – one hot noodle dish is called "ants climbing trees" – the inability to read them hardly ranks as a handicap. Point to what other people are eating if it looks good; most Chinese are welcoming and helpful, even in sign language.

3 **Do many Chinese speak English?**

C Very little, since the national bed-time is about 9pm – except in summer when people sit out in the street playing chess under street lamps. You may be offered a local opera or rather soppy ballet. I have yet to meet a tourist who can stand a whole Chinese opera; I have therefore seen considerably more beginnings than ends. The stories are often as batty as

Italian opera *libretti* and just as incomprehensible; but the costumes are glorious and audience participation total. Last May, I saw a Beijing opera version of *Othello* which was panned by the critics but still played to packed houses, where the audience rose to its collective feet in horror at Iago's treachery.

4 **When is the best time to go?**

D Once you have your permits, this is no great problem. If you are fearless, you can hire a bicycle; if you can count the stops, you can take a city bus: and if you have a cast-iron backside, you can take a country bus with baskets of fish and goats on the roof. Train tickets are sold at stations, usually just before departure; foreigners pay more than locals. Prices vary between the four classes: soft seat, soft sleeper, hard seat and hard sleeper. The soft class is very comfortable with four berths in a large compart-ment, antimacassars, Thermoses full of hot water, mugs for tea, and table-lamp. For over-night journeys, hard sleeper is also comfortable; long bunks in stacks of four fill the whole carriage, which is not divided into compartments.

5 **Is the food like Chinese food here?**

E In general, China is refreshingly free from the ritual and politeness you find in Japan; and the Chinese are basically very like us. But it should be remembered that China is a very puritanical country and misdemeanours involving local people will rebound on them very severely. There are some things western visitors find distasteful, like spitting. Some Chinese are aware of this, and when Chinese students were allocated rooms to share with foreigners at Beijing University, they were told not to spit on the floor as this might offend. So they would thoughtfully lean out and spit into the corridor.

6 Are there many places to eat?

F The most authentic restaurants in this country serve food similar to that in China; but they give no idea of the variety of Chinese cuisine, nor of its heights. The food served to foreigners in hotels (Western-style breakfast, Chinese lunch and dinner) is unexciting; so, particularly in areas like Sichuan where people are proud of their cooking, ask for special dishes in hotels or go out to eat.

Food in the North is best in winter when Mongolian hot-pot (slivers of mutton and vegetables, cooked in boiling soup in front of you) or heavy meat dumplings (*baozi*) help keep out the cold.

7 What sort of night-life is there?

G The Great Wall? The Forbidden City? There is so much to see in Beijing alone that every tourist complains of lack of time. In Beijing you should certainly get up early and take a taxi to the Marco Polo Bridge, and visit the Lama temple at lunchtime. But even the most unpromising places like industrial Wuhan and Zhengzhou have wonderful museums; and fantastic temples can be found in coal-blackened Datong and Taiyuan.

8 Is it easy to shop and where should I go?

H Silks of all sorts are very cheap in China, although the selection of patterns is not always as good as that offered in the Mainland China craft shop in Hong Kong. Silk can be bought by the metre, or ready-made into shirts, blouses, nightdresses (in a rather dated Thirties style) and petticoats or quilted jackets. Jewellery, of all sorts from jade and baroque pearls to lacquer or *cloisonné* beads, also makes a good present; again, however, the choice will vary.

9 What are the best things to bring back?

I You should take personal medicine and toilet articles with you, although you can buy most products in Beijing and Shanghai.

10 What should one do in an emergency?

J So many young people speak some English that it is practically impossible to be alone; keen students of English cluster round hotel gates in the hope of conversation.

11 What sights should I on no account miss?

K There are "Friendship Stores" in every city for foreigners. They stock a wide range of luxuries such as silk, jade, lacquer, *cloisonné* enamels as well as gym-shoes, leather brief-cases and biscuits. Shopping is easier in the Friendship Stores, but much more fun in the dimly-lit department stores full of T-shirts, enamel basins, inflatable plastic elephants and crowds of curious Chinese shoppers. If you see anything you like, buy it: you are unlikely ever to see the same patterned silk or jade carving in another city.

12 What are the medical facilities like?

L Foreigners are encouraged to stay in the more luxurious hotels where a double room with bathroom will cost from 30–50 yuan a night (about £10.20) exclusive of food.

The Chinese hotels which accept foreign "individual travellers" cost about six yuan a night in Beijing and are usually close to the railway station (and in Beijing can also be found near the smaller station at Yongding Gate). The dormitory rooms vary in size from about 10 beds upwards. Washing places are communal and there are none of the shops or facilities in the luxury hotels. Take mug and towel, as in the hard class on trains.

13 Is there anything special I should pack?

M October. But since the weather is then at its best throughout China, tourist facilities are stretched beyond capacity: you can expect to find 40 Venezuelans sleeping in the hotel lobby, but you cannot expect to find a taxi. Consider instead the crisp, sunny cold of North China in winter (and, in the same season, the balmy weather in Hong Kong), or risk the unpredictable climate in spring, and avoid queueing to see the Great Wall.

14 Are there any local rules of behaviour?

N No.

15 Should I ever offer tips?

O In large cities they are very good. But I do not recommend getting seriously ill in such distant parts as the Gobi Desert. Crises should be covered by travel insurance and if you are hospitalised with an acute problem you will be treated with Western medicines. The major problem encountered by tourists is the common cold, stronger in its Asian heartland than in the West. Though not very appetising, Chinese herbal remedies deal very effectively with colds; they can be obtained from any pharmacy or in hotel shops.

(Frances Wood in *The Sunday Times Colour Magazine*)

Reading for specific information

Working in pairs, find the answers to these questions. Don't spend more than two minutes on this exercise.

a) What's the cheapest kind of accommodation?
b) Is the weather in the North very different to that in the South?
c) Can I visit the countryside around Beijing on my own? If so, what's the best way to do it?
d) Am I likely to catch any illnesses? What can I do to cure them?
e) What opportunities are there to meet the people of China?
f) What's the food like? How do I order a meal?
g) What's the main unit of currency and what's its value in relation to the pound sterling?

Dealing with unfamiliar words

In each of the sentences below there are one or two words missing. They are all words which you may find difficult to understand. Without looking back at the passage, try and think of suitable words to fill the blanks. Note down any words in the context which help you.

a) '...and the Chinese are .... and helpful to foreigners. If you get lost, you are likely to be .... back to the hotel...' (paragraph A)
b) 'You may be offered (a visit to) a local opera or rather .... ballet. I have yet to meet a tourist who can stand a whole Chinese opera; (...) The stories are often as .... as Italian opera libretti and just as incomprehensible.' (paragraph C)
c) 'But it should be remembered that China is a very .... country and .... involving local people will rebound on them very severely.' (paragraph E)
d) 'But even the most .... places like industrial Wuhan and Zhengzhou have wonderful museums...' (paragraph G)
e) '...it is practically impossible to be alone; keen students of English .... round hotel gates in the hope of conversation.' (paragraph J)
f) 'Consider instead the crisp, sunny cold of North China in winter (and, in the same season, the .... weather in Hong Kong)...' (paragraph M)

Now look at the passage and check your answers. Did you guess correctly? If you didn't, do you understand the word in the passage? You can use your dictionary to check whether your answers mean more or less the same as the words in the passage.

Writing summaries

1 The passage contains advice on what the writer recommends the visitor to do and not to do. Complete the table below by summarising the information in the passage. Not all the boxes can be filled in.

	recommended	*not recommended*
transport		
sightseeing		
accommodation		
weather/seasons		
food		
restaurants		
entertainment		
shopping		
personal health and safety		

2 Now join your notes together in a paragraph summarising the passage in about 120 words.

Further work

1 Think how you would answer if you were being asked the same questions about your country. When you have prepared your answers, ask another student about his or her country and answer questions about your country.
If everybody in the class is from the same country, you can prepare answers about a country or a town you know well.

2 Look through the passage in this unit again and, if you have read them, the passages in units 16 and 17. Note down twenty words and expressions you have learnt. Using as much of the new vocabulary as possible, write a paragraph on one of the following subjects:
   – Describe your first visit to a foreign country.
   – Describe your country as seen through the eyes of a foreign visitor.
   – Describe your favourite town or country.

Unit 19   The capybara

Extracting main ideas

Read the passage and then choose the best summary.

The passage is about:
a) animals in captivity.
b) how delightful a capybara is.
c) how difficult it is to keep a capybara.
d) the writer's experiences with an unfamiliar animal.

With the arrival of the capybara things came to a head.

    A man led the huge rodent in on a string late one evening. It was half grown, very tame, and it sat there with an aloof and regal expression on its face while we bargained with its owner. The bargaining was protracted, for the owner had noticed the acquisitive   5 gleam in our eyes when we first beheld the beast, but at last the capybara was ours. He was housed in a large, coffin-shaped crate with a wire mesh front that seemed strong enough to withstand any onslaughts he might make upon it. We showered him with choice fruits and grasses, which he accepted with royal condescension, and   10 congratulated ourselves on having acquired such a lovely animal. We gazed at him spellbound while he ate, tenderly pressed a few more mangoes through the bars and went upstairs to sleep. We lay in the dark for a while, talking about our wonderful new specimen, and then eventually dozed off. At about midnight it began.   15

    I was awakened by a most curious noise coming from the garden beneath our window; it sounded like someone playing on a jew's harp accompanied rather erratically by someone else beating on a tin can. I was lying there listening to it, and wondering what it could be, when I suddenly remembered the capybara. With a cry of "the .20 capybara's escaping!" I leapt out of bed and fled downstairs to the garden, barefoot and in my pyjamas, closely followed by my drowsy companion. When we reached the garden all was quiet; the capybara was sitting on its haunches, looking down its nose in a superior manner. We had a long argument as to whether or not it was the   25 capybara that had been making the noise; I said it was and Smith said it was not. He insisted that the creature looked too calm and

innocent, and I maintained that that was exactly why I thought it was the culprit. The capybara just sat in its moonlit cage and stared through us. There was no repetition of the sound, so we went back to   30
bed, arguing in fierce whispers. No sooner had we settled down than the noise started again, and, if possible, it sounded louder than ever. I got out of bed and peered out of the window. The capybara cage was vibrating gently in the moonlight.

"It is that blasted animal," I said triumphantly.   35

"What's he doing?" enquired Smith.

"God knows, but we'd better go and stop him or he'll have the whole place awake."

We crept downstairs and from the shelter of a convenient cluster of bushes we surveyed the cage. The capybara was sitting by the wire   40
looking very noble. He would lean forward and place his enormous curved teeth round a strand of wire, pull hard and then release it so that the whole cage front vibrated like a harp. He listened until the noise had died away, and then he raised his large bottom and thumped his hind feet on the tin tray, making a noise like stage   45
thunder. I suppose he was applauding.

"Do you think he's trying to escape?" asked Smith.

"No, he's just doing it because he likes it."

The capybara played another little tune.

"Let's stop him, or he'll wake everyone."   50

"What can we do?"

"Remove the tin tray," said Smith practically.

"He'll still get that harpsichord effect with the wire."

"Let's cover the front of the cage up," said Smith.

So we removed the tray and covered the front of the cage with   55
sacks, in case it was the moonlight that was making the animal feel musical. He waited until we were in bed before he started twanging again.

(Gerald Durrell: *Three Singles to Adventure*)

Inferring

With another student, discuss what evidence there is in the passage to infer that:

a) the original owner of the capybara was asking a high price for the animal.
b) Smith and the writer were particularly pleased with their purchase.
c) they were concerned that the animal might try to escape.
d) the capybara only made the noise when it thought it wasn't being watched.
e) Smith and the writer were not living in complete isolation.
f) the writer assumes the animal liked the noise it was making.

Linking ideas

Note down:
a) all the nouns in the passage which refer to the capybara.
b) all the adjectives and adjectival expressions which refer to the cage.
c) all the words and expressions which refer to the noise the capybara makes.

Dealing with unfamiliar words

1 Write down all the words which mean the same as *looked* (*at*).

2 Some of the difficult words and expressions can be understood by looking at the context. Choose the best answers to the questions below.

   a) 'protracted' (line 5): This refers to (i) how long the bargaining took, (ii) how easy the bargaining was.
   Clue: The owner had seen how much the writer wanted to buy the animal.
   b) 'drowsy' (line 22): This is likely to mean (i) sleepy, (ii) slow.
   Clue: Smith and the writer had been wakened by the noise.
   c) 'haunches' (line 24): This probably refers to (i) part of the cage, (ii) part of the animal's body.
   Clue: How do rodents (e.g. rats) usually sit?
   d) 'cluster' (line 39): This refers to the (i) number of bushes, (ii) shape of the bushes.
   Clue: Did they want the animal to see them or not?
   e) 'twanging' (line 57): This probably refers to (i) the noise of the wire (ii) the noise of its feet on the tin tray.
   Clue: What does the word itself sound like? What was the first of the two sounds that the capybara made?

Understanding writer's style

a) The writer refers to the animal first of all as *it*, then as *he*. *He* is used:
   i)   when they noticed how large the animal was.
   ii) because they didn't know what sex the animal was at first.
   iii) because they became very fond of the animal, treating it more as a person.

b) Expressions like 'showered with choice fruit and grasses', and 'tenderly pressed a few more mangoes' suggest that:
   i)   the animal was very hungry.
   ii) the author and Smith were displaying their affection and interest.
   iii) the wire mesh front of the cage made it difficult to feed the animal.

c) The writer says 'I said triumphantly' because:
   i)   he was right and Smith was wrong.
   ii) he was pleased the animal was making the noise.
   iii) Smith wasn't sure whether the animal was making the noise.

Writing summaries

1 Decide which lines in the text the following headings refer to.

   a) How they obtained the capybara.
   b) What they did with the animal.
   c) What they did after feeding it.
   d) What happened at about midnight.
   e) What they did when they heard the noise.
   f) Why they were confused.
   g) Where the noise was coming from.
   h) What they did when the noise started again.
   i) How the capybara was making the noise.
   j) What they did to stop the capybara making the noise.
   k) What happened when they got back to bed.

2 Now, without looking back at the text, note down the answers to the headings.

3 Try and join your notes together in connected sentences using the following link words: *after, then, and, when, as soon as, before, so, but.*

4 Now look at the text and see if you have left any important information out. If you think it's absolutely essential, you can add it to your summary.

Further work

1 In fact, the capybara is the largest living rodent in the world, and lives in the tall grasslands along the streams and lakes in tropical South America.

   Choose an animal or a bird which you can find in your country. Write a short description of it. Think about size, habitat, food etc.

2 Choose ten to fifteen words and expressions from this passage. Write a paragraph describing an amusing or strange experience with an animal. You can make up the story if you like.

Unit 20 Save the jungle – save the world

Predicting

1 Look at the title of the unit. Discuss with another student what you might expect to find in the passage.

2 Now think of ten or so words that you might expect to find in this passage and write them down.

3 Read the passage and check whether the words you predicted in 2 appear or not.

A   The so-called Jungle of popular imagination, the tropical rain forest belt stretching around our planet at the Equator, has taken some 60 million years to evolve to its present state. It is, quite simply, the most complex, most important ecosystem on earth.

B   *Homo Faber*, Man the Builder, has tragically always seen the jungle as something alien, an environment to be vanquished, replaced with his own constructions. In the past twenty years the rate of pillage has increased alarmingly and huge tracts of verdant, beautiful forest—an irreplaceable treasure house of living things—has given way often, to wasteland. The evidence is that Man will redouble his destructive efforts until the forest 'system' is smashed, and the jungle will function no more.

C   Many experts gloomily predict that the tropical rain forests will finally vanish around the end of our century. Well done, 20th century!

D   What are the burning reasons that drive men to destroy our monumental inheritance?

E   Man seldom does anything for entirely rational reasons; usually, the less rational his 'reasons' the more he defends them with short-term economic arguments. That is one of the modern lessons in ecology.

F   *'We need the land for people,'* runs the argument. Well, many people already inhabit the tropical forest belt. There, native tribes have their own 'low-impact' life style, hunting, trapping, practising a little cultivation. Perhaps not idyllic, it is nevertheless a life style that does not endanger the forest ecosystem.

G   We stress a *little* cultivation because, paradoxically, the forest soil is often infertile; trees and green plants thrive on the compost of their fallen foliage, which is rapidly broken down and recycled as nutrients. So when the jungle is cleared to plant crops, there is no means of putting fertility back into the soil. Many governments spend much time 'resettling' people in deforested areas as part of so-called forward-looking development projects, but the crop yield is meagre, and brief: the soil soon makes its point. Erosion and flooding also tend to follow deforestation.

H   *'We need the timber; we need the animals for food, pelts and of course for sport,'* continues the argument.

I   Well, the forests have always been generous with their riches—so far as they are able. They are not limitless. They are being exhausted —*at ever-increasing speed*— and the habitats of innumerable other species of both flora and fauna are destroyed as a side effect.

J   Good husbandry—forest ecology, wisdom in planning, less greed and stupidity—could keep Man and the delicate rain forest relationship in balance indefinitely. This is our last great store house . . . our last wonderland.

(World Wildlife Fund)

K   Many of you will know—because you have already contributed to our efforts—that the World Wildlife Fund is currently supporting more than 30 important conservation projects in various rain forest areas alone. The Fund's 'Save the Tiger' appeal for £400,000 raised a magnificent £560,000, and governments responded not only by establishing reserves but also controlling the trade in skins.

L   Now we ask you to help us fund our biggest-ever international project: a two-year appeal to raise £½ million. The money will be used to sustain national parks and reserves within the tropical rain forest belt, in countries around the globe. Research, planning, manpower, equipment—all will be bought from the money you are able to give. If we cannot save the forests in their original state—and the axe, the bulldozer, and the greater and lesser bureaucrat with his deadly pen have already seen to that—we *must* save enough to preserve them as living burgeoning ecosystems—the most remarkable on earth.

Extracting main ideas

1 Choose the statement which gives the most accurate summary of the passage as a whole.

  a) The jungle could be saved if people take more care of it.
  b) Man defends his reasons for destroying the jungle with short-term economic arguments.
  c) The tropical rain forests of the world are disappearing and the World Wildlife Fund needs money to preserve them.
  d) The World Wildlife Fund is very successful with conservation projects.
  e) Deforestation of the jungle causes erosion and flooding.
  f) The riches of the jungle are limited and are being exhausted through Man's greed and stupidity.

⟫⟫→

2 According to the passage, the principal responsibility for the destruction of the jungle lies with:

   a) native tribes who live there.
   b) farmers who cultivate the land.
   c) the World Wildlife Fund.
   d) the authorities who claim they need the land and its resources.
   Note: two answers may be possible.

3 Look through the passage again and note down any suggestions it makes on how to save the jungle.

Dealing with unfamiliar words

1 A number of difficult words and expressions are explained either immediately afterwards or elsewhere in the passage. How are the following expressions explained?

   a) 'The so-called Jungle of popular imagination' (paragraph A)
   b) 'Homo Faber' (paragraph B)
   c) ' "low-impact" life style' (paragraph F)
   d) 'Good husbandry' (paragraph J)

2 What typographical devices (e.g. commas) are used to indicate that these expressions are being explained?

3 You may not understand the following words but they all have either a positive or a negative sense which you can guess from the context of the passage. Put a + or a − sign by each one according to its sense.

   a) 'alien' (paragraph B)   e) 'thrive' (paragraph G)
   b) 'pillage' (paragraph B)   f) 'meagre' (paragraph G)
   c) 'gloomily' (paragraph C)   g) 'burgeoning' (paragraph L)
   d) 'monumental' (paragraph D)

Linking ideas

1 What do the words in italics refer to?

   a) 'What are the burning reasons that drive men to destroy *our* monumental inheritance?' (paragraph D)
   b) '*We* need the timber; *we* need the animals. . .' (paragraph H)
   c) '*This* is our last great storehouse. . .' (paragraph J)

d) '. . .*you* have already contributed to *our* efforts. . .' (paragraph K)

e) 'If *we* cannot save the forests in their original state. . .' (paragraph L)

2 Find the following sentences in the passage and answer the questions.

a) '. . .the rate of pillage has increased alarmingly. . .' (paragraph B)
   Why is it alarming?

b) 'Many experts gloomily predict that. . .' (paragraph C)
   Why are the experts gloomy?

c) 'Perhaps not idyllic. . .' (paragraph F)
   Why isn't it idyllic?

d) '. . .the soil soon makes its point.' (paragraph G)
   What point does the soil make?

e) '. . .continues the argument.' (paragraph H)
   What argument?

f) '. . .both flora and fauna are destroyed as a side effect.' (paragraph I)
   As a side effect of what?

g) 'We must save enough to preserve them. . .' (paragraph L)
   Enough what?

Understanding writer's style

Work in groups of two or three.

1 What does the writer mean by writing 'Well done, 20th century!'?

2 In other places the writer uses extravagant and poetic language and images to convey the importance of the message.
   For example: '. . .an irreplaceable treasure house of living things' (paragraph B)
   Write down any other examples of this 'high' style.
   Why do you think the writer uses this style?
   a) Because the sound of the words is pleasing.
   b) In order to emphasise the message.
   c) Because the passage has been written in a hurry.

Further work

1 Working in groups of two or three, prepare a similar document entitled *either* 'Save our seas' *or* 'Save our countryside'.

2 Write down ten to fifteen words and expressions from the passage. Using as many of these as possible, write a paragraph or two describing the threat to a region of natural beauty in your country.

Unit 21   Beware the dirty seas

Reading for specific information

1 The following passage is about pollution in the Mediterranean. Imagine that you are planning a holiday on the Mediterranean coast. Read the passage through and note down the names of the places which you would be advised to avoid.

A   EVERY year 100 million holiday-makers are drawn to the Mediterranean. With one-third of the world's tourist trade, it is the most popular of all the holiday destinations: it is also the most polluted.

B   It has only 1 per cent of the world's sea surface, but carries more than half the oil and tar floating on the waters. Thousands of factories pour their poison into the Mediterranean, and almost every city, town and village on the coast sluices its sewage, un-treated, into the sea.

C   The result is that the Mediterranean, which nurtured so many civilisations, is gravely ill—the first of the seas to fall victim to the abilities and attitudes that evolved around it. And the pol-lution does not merely stifle the life of the sea—it threatens the people who inhabit and visit its shores.

D   Typhoid, paratyphoid, dysen-tery, polio, viral hepatitis and food poisoning are endemic in the area, and there are periodic out-breaks of cholera.

E   The mournful litany of disease is caused by sewage. Eighty-five per cent of the waste from the Mediterranean's 120 coastal cities is pushed out into the waters where their people and visitors bathe and fish. What is more, most cities just drop it in straight off the beach; rare indeed are the places like Cannes and Tel Aviv which pipe it even half a mile offshore.

F   Less than 100,000 of Greece's four million coastal people have their sewage properly treated—and Greece, as our map shows, is one of the cleaner countries of the northern shore.

G   The worst parts of the sea are the Israeli/Lebanon coast and be-tween Barcelona and Genoa, which flushes out over 200 tons of sewage each year for every mile of its length.

H   Not surprisingly, vast areas of the shallows are awash with bac-teria and it doesn't take long for these to reach people. Professor William Brumfitt of the Royal Free Hospital once calculated that anyone who goes for a swim in the Mediterranean has a one in seven chance of getting some sort of disease. Other scientists say this is an overestimate; but almost all of them agree that bathers are at risk.

I   An even greater danger lurks in the seductive seafood dishes that add so much interest to holiday menus. Shellfish are prime carriers of many of the most vicious diseases of the area.

J   They often grow amid pollution. And even if they don't they are frequently infected by the popular practice of 'freshening them up'—throwing filthy water over them in markets.

K   Industry adds its own poisons. Factories cluster round the coastline, and even the most modern rarely has proper waste-treatment plant. They do as much damage to the sea as sewage.

L   Fifteen thousand factories foul the Italian Ligurian riviera. Sixty thousand pollute the Tyrrhenian Sea between Sardinia, Sicily and the west Italian coast! The lagoon of Venice alone receives the effluents of 76 factories.

M   More filth comes washing down the rivers from industries far inland. The Po and the Rhone are the dirtiest, followed by the Ebro and the Llobregat in Spain, by the Adige and the Tiber in Italy, and by the Nile.

N   Thousands of tons of pesticides are blown off the fields into the sea, detergents from millions of sinks kill fish, and fertilisers, flushed out to sea, nourish explosions of plankton which cover bathers with itchy slime.

O   Then there is the oil—350,000 tons pouring each year from ships, 115,000 tons more from industries round the shore. Recent studies show that the Mediterranean is four times as polluted by oil as the north Atlantic, 40 times as bad as the north-east Pacific.

P   Apart from the nine-mile-wide Strait of Gibraltar, the Mediterranean is landlocked, virtually unable to cleanse itself. It takes 80 years for the water to be renewed, through the narrow, shallow straits, far too slow a process to cope with the remorseless rush of pollution.

Q   Weak coastal currents keep sewage and industrial waste close to the shore and gently spin floating oil and tar towards the beaches. And the sea's feeble tides can do little to help remove it.

R   Of course, the people of the Mediterranean have always used the sea for their wastes. The canals of Venice, the waters of the Bosphorous and the sea off the Nile Delta have been health hazards for centuries.

S   But the population has increased round the shores to 100 million and a further 100 million tourists come annually. The population of the French and Italian rivieras trebles every summer.

T   Three tourists visit the northern shore every year for every yard of beach. With the numbers of holidaymakers expected to double in the next 20 years, it is hard for even the best treatment plants to cope.

U   The good news is that the countries of the Mediterranean have been coming together to work out how to save their common sea.

V   But it will be a long time before the measures they approved take effect in cleaning up the sea.

(Geoffrey Lean in *The Observer*)

»»→

2 The passage contains a number of statistics and facts. Read the passage again and complete the chart below. Some of the statistics you will have to calculate yourself. Check your answers with another student.

Facts about the Mediterranean	*Facts about pollution in the Mediterranean*

coastal population:
number of tourists/year:
ratio of population to
   tourists:
percentage of world tourist
   trade:
percentage of world's sea
   surface:
number of coastal cities:
	percentage of world's sea pollution:
	percentage of sewage which is untreated:
	number of factories polluting:
	  – Ligurian Riviera:
	  – Tyrrhenian Sea:
	  – Venice lagoon:
	tons of oil/year from:
	  – ships:
	  – factories:

Checking comprehension

Discuss with another student whether the symbols on the map below representing the extent of pollution in the Mediterranean are in the right position according to the information given in the passage.

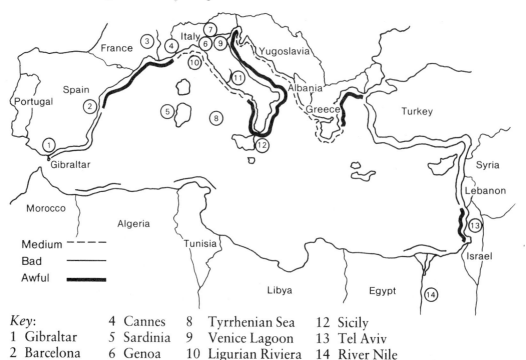

Key:
1 Gibraltar
2 Barcelona
3 River Rhone

4 Cannes
5 Sardinia
6 Genoa
7 River Po

8 Tyrrhenian Sea
9 Venice Lagoon
10 Ligurian Riviera
11 River Tiber

12 Sicily
13 Tel Aviv
14 River Nile

Inferring

Although the passage contains many factual points of information, the writer uses them to point out the dangers to the inhabitants and visitors in the Mediterranean region. However, he does not give any specific advice. What advice for tourists can you infer from the passage?

Example: Avoid eating shellfish unless you know that it is fresh and has been farmed in unpolluted waters.

Writing summaries

1 The passage begins with a general statement that the Mediterranean is the most polluted sea in the world. It then lists the various causes and consequences of the pollution, and mentions a number of geographic and demographic (to do with the distribution of population and industry) factors. Make a list of all these points mentioned in the passage.

   Example: Causes: untreated sewage
             Consequences: various diseases
             Other factors: coastal industries

2 Write a summary of the passage in no more than 120 words by joining the notes made in the exercise above into connected sentences.

Further work

1 There are very few areas in the world which are not affected by pollution, and we all contribute to it in many ways. Think about environmental pollution in the town where you live and ways to reduce it. Working in groups of two or three, prepare a report and present it to the others in the class.

2 Look through the passage again and, if you have read them, the passages in units 19 and 20. Note down twenty or so words and expressions which you have learnt. Using as much of this new vocabulary as possible, write a paragraph or two on one of the following subjects:
   – Household pets.
   – Hunting.
   – Conserving wildlife.

Unit 22   The sword that can heal

This passage concerns the uses being made of the laser, which is a device for concentrating light waves into an intense beam of light.

Extracting main ideas

1 Read the passage through quickly and decide which of the headings below describes the general theme of the passage.
   – Military uses for the laser.
   – Cancer surgery.
   – Surgical uses for the laser.
   – New technology in British hospitals.

2 Match the following headings to the paragraphs.
   a) Treating cancer
   b) Ear surgery and dentistry
   c) Cosmetic surgery
   d) The pin-point accuracy of the laser
   e) The laser as a powerful surgical instrument
   f) The laser in British hospitals

Understanding text organisation

Read the passage through again slowly. In each paragraph there is one sentence which doesn't belong. When you have finished reading, note down the line numbers of these sentences.
Check your answers with another student.

A WHILE military scientists test lasers against satellites, surgeons use them as miraculously accurate scalpels. They can even be used to detonate
5 hydrogen bombs. The beam can be focused to spot one fiftieth the size of a human hair; yet its intensity is enough to kill cancer cells or drill through the most delicate bones.

B   More than a decade ago, eye surgeons realised that they could use the laser's beam to seal individually, the microscopic blood vessels in the retina. The beam is so fine that only the
15 target is heated. Now its pin-point blasting power has been turned to destroying cancer cells and reducing birthmarks. For cancer treatment, the diseased cells must be killed while
20 their healthy neighbours are left unharmed. Where the cancer can be directly and accurately attacked, laser treatment does well: early cancer of the cervix and skin cancers have been
25 widely and successfully treated. This type of cancer is not very easy to reach. For cancers that are less accessible, there is a new and potentially valuable technique in which the
30 patient is injected with a chemical that then attaches itself preferentially to cancer cells. When the laser strikes the chemical, it releases a form of oxygen that kills these cells.

C   The marvellous accuracy of the surgical laser can be increased by sending the beam along fibres of glass far finer than a human hair. The "optical fibres" carry it around cor-
40 ners and direct it precisely at a tiny area; so little of the beam spills from the glass that there is no risk of damaging healthy cells. This technique is particularly useful in ear
45 surgery.

Furthermore, the laser beam can D also remove bone, and so it is invaluable in ear surgery. The sounds we hear are carried from the eardrum to the nerves of the ear by a delicate set 50 of pivoting bones which sometimes solidify, causing deafness. A laser beam vaporises the bone without touching any of the surrounding tissue. The beam is diffused to avoid 55 scarring and the mark becomes inconspicuous. This accuracy in targeting makes the laser a useful tool for the dentist also – a nerve can be reached through a hole drilled in the 60 enamel.

Birthmarks, once almost untreat- E able, are a mass of blood vessels and, being red, they absorb the laser beam strongly. It seals them so that the 65 mark becomes less conspicuous. The normal cells of the skin's surface, which don't absorb much of the laser beam, act in the healing and help to conceal the mark. The beam can cut 70 with a precision that no scalpel could achieve. The operation can transform the lives of people who were previously doomed to a lifetime of cosmetic concealment. 75

Though this application is widely F used in America, there are in Britain only two hospitals offering the treatment, and one feels bound to warn patients that success is not certain. 80 However, some 10 new centres will soon be opened. Britain, though, is one of the leaders in the laser treatment of bleeding peptic ulcers and this, combined with new medicines 85 can mean ulcer treatment without conventional surgery. The laser is now being used to treat all kinds of illnesses in this country.

(Tony Osman in *The Sunday Times Colour Magazine*)

Dealing with unfamiliar words

You would usually expect to find the words below only in the specialised context of medical matters, so you may find them difficult to understand. But there are one or two clues to their meanings either in the immediate context or elsewhere in the passage.

a) 'scalpel' (lines 3 and 71)
Example: a) 'scalpel' – 'cut' (line 70), 'precision' (line 71)
So it's probably something which cuts with precision. What do surgeons use?

Look for clues to the meaning of the other words. Try and work out their general sense.

b) 'retina' (line 13)
c) 'optical fibres' (line 39)
d) 'enamel' (line 61)
e) 'blood vessels' (lines 13 and 63)

Writing summaries

1 Go through the passage again and complete the chart below. Not every space can be filled in from the information given; if this is the case, just leave a blank. Note that various answers are acceptable and can be expressed in different ways.

What the laser is used to treat	How it is used	Advantages of using the laser
1 retina		
2	destroys diseased cells	
3 deafness		does not touch any of the surrounding tissue
4		
5 peptic ulcers		

2 Without looking back at the passage, make sentences by joining all the notes in
   the chart together.
   Example: The laser can be used to treat the retina by sealing the blood vessels.
            The advantage is that only the target is heated.

3 When you have finished, re-read the passage quickly to see if you have left
   anything out of your summary.

Further work

1 Work in groups of two or three. Choose one of the following topics and find out
   how the laser can be used:

   – telecommunications   – defence
   – space research   – shopping
   – entertainment   – industry

   Prepare a short talk on your topic. You may use reference books, including
   dictionaries, to help you prepare your talk. When you are ready, give your talk to
   the rest of the class.

2 Note down ten to fifteen useful words and expressions from the passage. Use
   them in a paragraph describing an illness or an operation which you or one of
   your family has had.

Unit 23   How to live to be a hundred

Understanding text organisation

1 In the passage opposite there are a number of sentences missing. Read it through and decide where the sentences below should go.

a) But it is important to make a distinction between calmly relaxed and passively lazy.

b) Puritanical arguments about smoking and drinking have little to support them.

c) People who want a long life with an alert old age should never retire.

d) But, in gaining success, individuals should not overstress themselves.

e) A sense of humour, impishness, a feeling that life is fun, are strong weapons against ageing.

f) Such activities as walking and gardening prolong life spectacularly because they are 'non-intensive' forms of all-over bodily movement.

g) That does not imply a harsh military-style masochism but the ordering of life and the imposition of a pattern on the events of the day.

2 In the passage there are a number of statements made by the writer concerning what you have to do to live a long life. These statements are sometimes modified by counter arguments.
For example: paragraph 2
> Some people are naturally more physically active than others, and are at a considerable advantage providing their activities are not the result of stress.
> *but* If they take exercise too seriously, it will work against them.

Re-read the passage and note down any other statements and counter arguments. Remember that some will be signalled by words such as *but*, others will not be signalled at all.

For adults who remain vivaciously childlike in old age, there has to be a sustained enthusiasm for some aspect of life. (1) .... If they are forcibly retired they should immerse themselves in some new, absorbing activity.

Some people are naturally more physically active than others, and are at a considerable advantage providing their activities are not the result of stress. (2) .... The more earnest ageing exercisers display a conscious or unconscious anxiety about their health. If they take exercise too seriously it will work against them. Older individuals who take up intensive athletic activity are usually people who fear declining health. Yet it is crucial that physical exercise – as we grow past the young sportsman stage – should be extensive rather than intensive and, above all, *fun*.

A calm temperament favours longevity. Those who are sharply aggressive, emotionally explosive or naggingly anxious are at a grave disadvantage. (3) .... Relaxation does not contradict the idea of passionate interest. Indeed, zest for living, eagerness to pursue chosen subjects are vital in long life.

Thinking about 'the good old days', complaining about how the world is deteriorating, criticising the younger generations, are sure signs of an early funeral.

Being successful is a great life-stretcher, and can even override such life-shorteners as obesity and fondness for drink. (4) .... And success must always be measured in personal terms. A hill-shepherd may feel just as successful in his own way as a Nobel Laureate.

Long-lived individuals seem to be more concerned with what they *do* than who they *are*. They live outside themselves rather than dwelling on their own personalities.

In personal habits, the long-lived are generally moderate. Extremes of diet are not common. A mixed diet seems to favour longevity. (5) .... Many long-lived individuals enjoy nicotine and alcohol – in moderation.

Most long-lived people have a sense of self-discipline. (6) .... The man who lives long because he walks a mile a day does so because he does it *every* day, as part of an organised existence.

Over and over, during my researches, it emerged that long life goes with a "twinkle in the eye". (7) .... The sour-faced puritan and the solemn bore soon begin to lose ground, leaving their more amused contemporaries to enjoy the last laugh.

Finally, nothing is to be gained by a head-in-the-sand avoidance of the facts of life and death. The healthiest solution is to accept that one's span on Earth is limited and then to live every day, *in the present*, and to the full.

(Desmond Morris: *The Book of Ages*)

Dealing with unfamiliar words

1 The words on the left may be unfamiliar to you. Use the clues on the right to help you understand what they mean. Check your answers with another student.

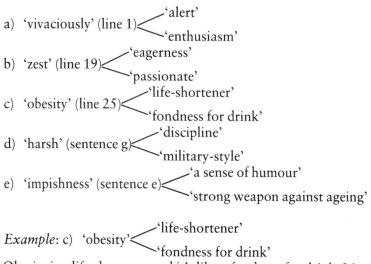

a) 'vivaciously' (line 1) — 'alert' / 'enthusiasm'

b) 'zest' (line 19) — 'eagerness' / 'passionate'

c) 'obesity' (line 25) — 'life-shortener' / 'fondness for drink'

d) 'harsh' (sentence g) — 'discipline' / 'military-style'

e) 'impishness' (sentence e) — 'a sense of humour' / 'strong weapon against ageing'

Example: c) 'obesity' — 'life-shortener' / 'fondness for drink'

Obesity is a life-shortener and it's like a fondness for drink. It's probably something to do with a fondness for some other life-shortener e.g. smoking or eating too much food.
Can you now guess the meaning of obesity?

Use the same techniques for any other words which you don't know.
Check your answers.

2 The writer uses a number of images to describe particular characteristics or attitudes:

a) 'an early funeral' (line 23)
b) 'a great life-stretcher' (line 24)
c) 'a twinkle in the eye' (line 41)
d) 'the sour-faced puritan' (lines 41–2)
e) 'a head-in-the-sand avoidance' (lines 45–6)

Choose their probable meanings from the list below.

i)   enthusiasm and youthful spirits
ii)   a shortened life
iii) a refusal to face reality
iv) a love of alcohol and food
v)   someone who is morally very strict

vi)   a good way of living longer
vii) ignorance and narrow-mindedness
viii) fondness for practical jokes
ix)   shyness and nervousness

Writing summaries

1 Make a list of things which the writer recommends as important for a long life.

   Example: You should: have enthusiasm for some aspect of life
                          be physically active

2 Now think of examples of the kinds of things which the writer might
   recommend you to do or not to do.
   Join the notes you made in 1 into connected sentences using phrases to signal
   examples, such as *for example, for instance, an example of this is. . ., such as. . .*

   Example: For instance, you should go walking and do gardening.

Further work

1 Do you think your present life style will allow you to live a long life? In groups of
   three or four discuss what you should change in your life styles in order to live
   longer.

2 It has been predicted that within the next 50 years, scientists will have produced
   a drug to prolong life up to 150 years or more. What effects will this have on
   society? Think about:

   – marriage and divorce   – jobs
   – food   – physical effects of old age
   – room to live   – population

   Imagine that the government is about to legalise the use of this drug. Prepare
   your arguments for or against the proposed law, and present them to the other
   students in a class debate.

3 Choose ten to fifteen words and expressions from the passage and write a
   paragraph describing *either* an old person you know *or* how you expect to cope
   with old age.

Unit 24   How to help the hard of hearing

Predicting

1 Look at the title of this unit. Think of ten to fifteen words which you are likely to find in the passage.

2 Working with another student, think of two or three ways in which you can help the hard of hearing.

3 As you read the passage, answer the questions. Try not to look at the rest of the passage. Check your answers with another student.

> A   People who begin to go deaf in adult life have different problems from those who are born deaf.

a) So what sort of problems do you think they have?

> They have to learn different ways of behaving and different ways of communicating – perhaps at a time when learning is not all that easy.

> B   A hearing aid is not a complete solution to the problem.

b) Why do you think the hearing aid isn't a complete solution?

> The sound perceived by the deaf person through a hearing aid is distorted and appears to have more background noise than is heard by someone with normal hearing.

c) How can they cope with this?

> Deafened people have to lipread as well.

> C   Lipreading is difficult, demands intense concentration, and an uninterrupted direct view of the speaker's face.

d) So what do you think the lipreader has to do to make it easier?

No other activities can take place at the same time: the lipreader has to stop eating, stop reading, stop washing up, stop mending, stop everything in order to concentrate on hearing. It is not a question of stupidity or bad temper – as it sometimes appears to be – but a question of being very easy to misunderstand when the sound is distorted. Remember what it's like trying to communicate on a very bad telephone line.

e) So what is communicating on a very bad telephone line like?

Frustrating, isn't it? The deaf have to face that all the time.

D   A useful way of looking at the problem is to see the deaf person as a foreigner – to treat them as if you were in a foreign country.

f) What would you do to make it easier to communicate with a foreigner?

You would speak more clearly, slowly and raise your voice slightly. And you'd use gestures to make your meaning clear, as well as have no hesitation in using pencil and paper to be absolutely certain. You can do all those things with the deaf – as well as making sure you don't obscure your mouth with your hand, a pipe, or a cigarette.

g) Can you think of any other situations in which the hearing aid is less effective?

E   Another point quite often overlooked is that a hearing aid may be quite useful in a quiet carpeted room – but try it in the High Street in the rush hour, in a noisy car, in a railway station ticket office, a cinema or a concert hall and you've got a really difficult problem to distinguish speech. So don't suggest to or encourage deaf people to go to functions which are going to make their disability appear worse – and increase their sense of failure.

h) Is there anything you can do to help deaf people either in the home or in the situations mentioned in paragraph E?

F   On the other hand careful selection of cinemas with good sound systems is important and you should experiment to find out where the best seats are for hearing, fitting adaptors for radio and television, observing which friends are easier to understand, and making sure that people talking are well-lit are all useful and positive activities.

(Health Education Council)

4 How many of the words you predicted in 1 appeared in the passage?
   Did it mention all the ways of helping deaf people which you thought of in 2?

Extracting main ideas

1 Decide which of the statements below present the main ideas of complete
   paragraphs, and which ones summarise only part of a paragraph.

   a) Pencil and paper will help you communicate with deaf people.
   b) If you were talking to a foreigner you'd speak clearly and use gestures.
   c) Deaf people can get frustrated in places where their hearing aids don't work
       so well.
   d) Hearing aids are not very efficient in noisy places.
   e) A deaf person has to lipread even when using a hearing aid.
   f) Deaf people sometimes appear stupid and bad-tempered.
   g) A lipreader can't do two things at once.
   h) People who lose their hearing have to learn new ways of communicating.
   i) It's a good idea to express yourself as if you were talking to a foreigner.
   j) Deaf people can't lipread if you obscure your mouth.
   k) You can help deaf people by being sensitive about their surroundings.

2 Match the statements with the paragraphs they refer to. Check your answers
   with another student.

Linking ideas

Look at the following sentences and answer the questions.

a) '. . .appears to have more background noise. . .' (paragraph B)
    What appears to have more background noise?
b) 'It's not a question of stupidity or bad temper. . .' (paragraph C)
    What isn't?
c) 'The deaf have to face that all the time.' (paragraph C)
    Face what?
d) '. . .using pencil and paper to be absolutely certain.' (paragraph D)
    To be certain of what?
e) '. . .are all useful and positive activities.' (paragraph F)
    Useful for doing what?

Inferring

a) In paragraph C, why should it sometimes appear to be a question of stupidity or bad temper?
b) In paragraph E, 'another point overlooked' suggests that something has been overlooked before this. What?
c) In paragraph E, why might you increase deaf people's sense of failure?
d) In paragraph F, why should you make sure people talking are well-lit?

Writing summaries

1 Re-read the passage and make a checklist of things which you should do when you are with a deaf person.
   When you have finished, check the passage to make sure you have left nothing out.

2 Working in groups of two or three, prepare a list of things you could include in a leaflet specially written for people who have just become deaf. Explain some of the things they should try to do, and what they should ask other people to do to help them.

Further work

1 It is quite common to find people who are hard of hearing in a foreign language class. What kind of problems do they have when learning a foreign language, and what sort of things can you, your teacher, and your school do to help them? Make a list of your recommendations and discuss them with another group.

2 How well equipped is your school to receive students who are disabled in other ways? Can you think of any improvements to the school?

3 Look through this passage again and, if you have read them, the passages in units 22 and 23. Note down twenty words or expressions which you have learnt. Using as much of this new vocabulary as possible, write a paragraph on one of the following subjects:

   – If you had one million pounds to spend on medical research, what would you spend it on?
   – Keeping fit.
   – Advice on how to help the blind.

Unit 25   Sorry sir, sorry, sorry

Understanding text organisation

1 In the following passage there are three sentences which are in the wrong
   position. Decide which they are and where they should go.

2 The sentences and the numbers on the plan below describe the different stages
   the writer had to go through before buying a ticket. Match the sentences to the
   numbers.

   a) Went to supervisor. Told to go back to ticket sales.
   b) Went to buy ticket. Told to go to ticket sales.
   c) Explained the problem. Told to buy another ticket.
   d) Went to ticket sales. Told plane was full. Booked flight for next day.
   e) Went to ticket sales. Waited about one hour.
   f) Went to supervisor. Told to buy another ticket.

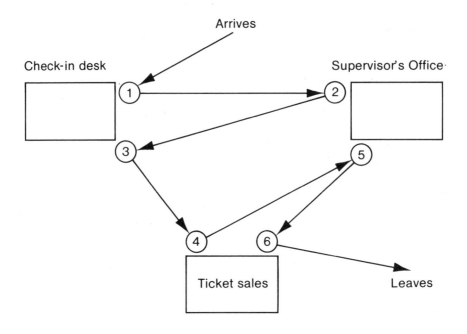

The moral of Victor Keegan's story would be Don't Fly Pan Am—if only the other airlines were any better.

"WE'VE got a small problem," I said to the man at the Pan Am check-in desk in Washington. "I'm booked in on this flight to London, but I've only today discovered that they tore off the Washington to London part of the ticket on the shuttle from New York, leaving the shuttle ticket still here."

"That's all right," he said, "you'll just have to buy another ticket."

"I beg your pardon."

"You will have to buy another ticket."

"You're joking."

"No sir, that's the rules."

"But I booked on this flight. You can see from the front of the schedule. And presumably my details are in the computer. I can't possibly have used the ticket because the flight hasn't gone yet."

Knowing a brick wall when I am speaking to one, I joined the other queue for tickets and, with less than an hour for take-off, I was standing no. 3 behind a group of youths and a lady from Yugoslavia with her family.

"No, but someone else could use it. Sorry, there's nothing I can do about it."

"Can I see the supervisor?"

"You can, but he will say exactly the same thing. He's round the corner. I'll keep a place here for you."

I went back to my place at the front of the queue and asked, reluctantly, for a ticket. After a long discussion, if that's the right word, with the supervisor (who did make an attempt to ring Eastern Airlines to see if they had filed the mistake) I was told there was

no alternative but to purchase a ticket and claim it back later.

"Sorry, sir," he said, "I can't sell you a ticket, this is bookings only. You'll have to go down there to the ticket sales counter."

"But you told me to come back here."

"Sorry, I cannot sell you a ticket from here."

The trouble was the computer, which was having a problem and could not call up the details of the lady's booking. Not for five minutes. Not for ten minutes. Nor even after 50 minutes when the plane was about to take off. Every attempt to try to book at another desk was met with the answer, "We can't deal with new tickets until all the bookings have been dealt with." Back to the supervisor. No luck. One of his deputies said, "Don't worry, you will get on."

When my temper had cooled, I booked a flight out on the next flight the following morning via New York (cost 474 dollars).

With the plane five minutes' overdue for take-off, I finally got a vacant ticket desk.

"One single to London, please."

"Sorry, sir, the plane is full up."

"It's what?"

"Full up."

For the umpteenth time, I recounted my story. "Do you really mean I can't even pay twice for a ticket I am already in the computer as having booked?"

"Sorry, sir, nothing I can do about it."

It would be too simple to say that the moral of all this is "Fly Pan Am. You'll never forget the experience" – because other airlines apparently have similar rules. But the benefits to the casual traveller of checking tickets regularly need not be understated.

(Victor Keegan in *The Guardian*)

Checking comprehension

Decide whether the following statements are true or false.

a) The writer wanted to go back to London via New York.
b) They took the wrong part of the ticket on the New York–Washington flight.
c) The writer thought it would be simple to rectify the error.
d) The man at the check-in desk thought the supervisor would be able to help.
e) The writer was told to buy a new ticket and then look for the one torn off by mistake.
f) The writer did not have to queue a second time at the check-in desk.
g) The writer had to wait in a long queue at the ticket sales desk.
h) The supervisor reassured the writer that he would get on the plane.
i) Fortunately for the writer, the plane's departure was delayed.
j) Because the plane was overbooked, the writer had to spend the night in New York.

Inferring

What evidence is there in the passage for the following statements?

a) Each stage of a journey involving several flights is represented by a separate part of the ticket.
b) You are not allowed to take a flight if you do not have the relevant part of the ticket.
c) Even though the airline computer records your name and details of your flights, there is no proof that you have the ticket, unless you actually have it in your possession.
d) If an airline realises a mistake has been made, it will not necessarily try and contact the passenger or the other airlines concerned.
e) If you have to buy a second ticket, the airline will reimburse you when the mistake has been cleared up.
f) If a flight is not fully booked, you can buy a ticket just before the plane leaves.
g) You cannot buy tickets from the check-in desk.
h) All passengers who have booked tickets must check in before any new tickets for that flight can be sold.
i) This kind of problem is not restricted to Pan Am.

Linking ideas

Answer the following questions.

a) '. . .that they tore off the Washington to London part. . .' (lines 11–12)
   Who did?

b) '. . .leaving the shuttle ticket still here.' (lines 14–15)
   Where?

c) 'No sir, that's the rules.' (line 23)
   What are the rules?

d) 'And presumably my details are in the computer.' (lines 26–7)
   What kind of details?

e) 'Sorry, there's nothing I can do about it.' (lines 40–1)
   About what?

f) '. . .but he will say exactly the same thing.' (lines 43–4)
   So what will he say?

g) 'I'll keep a place here for you.' (lines 45–6)
   Where?

h) '. . .but to purchase a ticket and claim it back later.' (lines 56–7)
   Claim what back?

i) 'But you told me to come back here.' (lines 63–4)
   Come back where?

j) 'Don't worry, you will get on.' (lines 81–2)
   Get on what?

k) '. . .the moral of all this is. . .' (line 105)
   The moral of all what?

Understanding complex sentences

1 Choose one of the following sentences which have been printed without
   punctuation. Read it to another student, pausing in suitable places. Then answer
   the questions.

   a) After a long discussion if that's the right word with the supervisor who did
      make an attempt to ring Eastern Airlines to see if they had filed the mistake I
      was told there was no alternative but to purchase a ticket and claim it back
      later.
      i)   Who told the writer what to do?
      ii) What did the supervisor do?
      iii) When was the writer told what to do?   ⟫→

111

b) Knowing a brick wall when I am speaking to one I joined the other queue for tickets and with less than an hour for take-off I was standing no. 3 behind a group of youths and a lady from Yugoslavia with her family.
   i)   Where was the lady?
   ii) Where were the youths from?
   iii) Did the writer speak to anyone in the queue?
   iv) At what time did the writer join the queue?

2 Choose one of the extracts and re-write it more simply. Make sure you extract the main ideas and use less complex sentence structures.

Understanding writer's style

Answer the following questions.

a) The writer said 'We've got a small problem' (line 6) because:
   i)   he was travelling with someone.
   ii) he thought it was Pan Am's and the writer's problem.
   iii) he was really being ironic; he was sure it was Pan Am's problem.

b) The man at the check-in desk said 'That's all right.' (line 16) to show that:
   i)   Pan Am didn't think it would be a problem.
   ii) Pan Am didn't think it was their problem.
   iii) it wasn't the writer's problem.

c) The writer wrote 'Knowing a brick wall when I am speaking to one. . .' (line 31):
   i)   because he realised he couldn't buy a ticket at this desk.
   ii) because it was difficult to talk in the noisy airport building.
   iii) because the bookings clerk was unhelpful and unresponsive.

d) The writer wrote 'After a long discussion, *if that's the right word*. . .' (lines 50–1):
   i)   to suggest that the writer can't think of the right word.
   ii) to indicate that his conversation with the supervisor was not as calm as the word usually suggests.
   iii) to suggest that it wasn't really a discussion because the supervisor was helpful and rang up Eastern Airlines.

Further work

1 Look back at the passage in this unit and choose ten to fifteen words or expressions. Use them in a description of the most complicated or frustrating journey you have ever made.

2 All sorts of criticisms are made about airlines, such as high prices, complex fare structures, poor food, delays etc. Working in groups of two or three make a list of as many criticisms as you can think of. Then discuss which three are the most serious. Check your list of criticisms with others in the class. Find out which are the three criticisms that everyone agrees on.

Unit 26   Go steady on the gas!

Extracting main ideas

Read the introduction to the passage quickly, and choose the best title from the list below. Don't worry if there are some words which you don't understand at the moment.

— Driving in California
— Fuel saving in town
— Get 25% more mpg!*
— Gas consumption in the USA
— On your way in the USA!

* mpg: miles per gallon

> From snow-clogged mountain roads to desert highways, freeways to
> congested city streets, Californians face a variety of tough driving
> conditions. But thanks to savvy driving, they consume proportionately
> less gasoline than the rest of the nation. Here, some tips from the
> 5 Golden State that will help drivers all over the country to get up to 25%
> more miles per gallon! By SUSAN NESTOR

Predicting

1 Before you read the rest of the passage, decide which of the following words you would expect to find in the passage, and in what sort of context. If you don't understand all the words, check their meanings in a dictionary. Don't forget that some of the words may be either American or British English usage.

friction	trunk	lane	traffic
air conditioner	evaporation	petrol	boot
sea level	bonnet	brakes	
gas	chains	hood	

2 Now think of three ways in which you could use less petrol.

3 Read the passage and check whether the words you chose in 1 appeared or not. Which words might have appeared but didn't?

FREEWAY FRENZY

● **Try to maintain a steady speed—** especially on freeways and ex-
10 pressways. Never exceed a steady 55 mph. Varying speed by as lit-tle as 5mph can reduce mileage by 1.5 miles per gallon. Avoid constant lane changes to "get
15 ahead."

● **Buy radial tires.** If you do a lot of expressway driving, they can increase mileage by as much as 10%. Your fuel savings will de-
20 fray the higher tire price.

ON CITY STREETS

● **Plan your route.** City driving consumes about 50% more fuel than highway driving (100%
25 more in congested traffic). Al-ways opt for a route with syn-chronized traffic signals to get the best run for your money.

● **Avoid unnecessary braking.** An-
30 ticipate traffic light changes; it takes a lot of extra gas to get the car up to speed again.

● **Avoid streets with bad pavement.** Stop-and-go weaving can up gas
35 usage by 20%. Instead, take a slightly longer route on a better road.

HOT TIMES...

● **Gas up early in the day,** es-
40 pecially in hot weather. Gasoline expands as it gets hot—the more it expands, the less you get. Bet-ter to have it expand in your tank than in the gas pump.

45 ● **Using the air conditioner cuts mileage by 13%-20%,** but high-speed driving with the windows open can rob even more mpg. Use the air conditioner only long
50 enough to cool the car.

● **Keep your car in a garage,** or park in a shady spot. Hot-weather evaporation can siphon off as much as a quart of gas a day.

...AND COLD

55 ● **In winter, keep the car in a ga-rage.** It will start up easier, and start-up time is when you use the most gasoline. No garage? Cover the engine compartment with an
60 old blanket or rug to shield it from cold winds; *remove* before starting up.

● **Scrape off all ice and snow.** Driving in snow consumes more
65 gas anyway; no sense hauling around extra weight.

● **Snow tires create more friction than regular tires and take away 2-3 mpg.** Don't put them on un-
70 til necessary and change them as soon as the snow season ends. Tire chains are even worse; use them only in extreme conditions.

● **Have your mechanic use a**
75 **lighter-grade gear lubricant.** It will warm up faster, easing fric-tion and saving gas.

UPS AND DOWNS

● **Mountain driving.** Going up a 3°
80 grade decreases mpg by 32%, a 7° grade by 55%. When ap-proaching a long uphill grade, gradually increase speed to build up momentum for the climb.
85 Keep the car in high gear until the engine starts to strain, then shift to a lower gear to complete the ascent.

● **When going downhill, use the**
90 **brakes rather than a lower gear** to control speed except on long, steep downhill runs, where brakes might burn out.

● **High-altitude driving cuts gas**
95 **mileage 4% for every 1,000 feet above sea level.** If you regularly drive above 5,000 feet, have your carburetor adjusted for a leaner gasoline-air mix.   ■

(Susan Nestor, reprinted from the May 10th, 1983 issue of *Family Circle Magazine.* © 1985 The Family Circle, Inc.)

Dealing with unfamiliar words

1 Write down all the words which refer to parts of the car or accessories. Decide what they mean or what you think the parts do. Check your answers with another student.

Example: 'tank' (line 43)
  – noun
  – something you can put gasoline in
  – 'your tank' suggests it belongs to the car
  – probably the part of the car which holds the petrol

2 Choose the most likely answer.

a) 'snow-clogged' (line 1): (i) cleared of snow, (ii) blocked by snow
   Clue: The passage deals with how to save petrol and gives a few examples of the driving conditions which can increase your fuel consumption. Look at the other examples.

b) 'congested' (line 2): (i) busy, (ii) empty
   Clue: What kind of driving conditions do you usually find in a city?

c) 'savvy' (line 3): (i) thoughtless, (ii) intelligent
   Clue: Californians use less fuel than the average driver. How do you think they manage to do this?

d) 'defray' (line 19): (i) help pay for, (ii) not pay for
   Clue: Radial tyres can save you money, but they cost more. However, the passage recommends that you buy this kind of tyre. Why?

e) 'synchronized traffic signals' (line 26): traffic lights which (i) change frequently, (ii) work in sequence
   Clue: Which kind is likely to help save you petrol?

f) 'stop-and-go weaving' (line 34): (i) steering the car slowly round the holes in the road, (ii) driving at a steady speed
   Clue: Bad pavements are something to avoid because they cause this kind of driving.

3 American English sometimes differs from British English in its vocabulary. If you don't come across examples of American English very often, you may not understand some of the words in the passage. Work in pairs and try to match the American English words (US) on the left with their British counterparts (GB) on the right. There are some words which are not in the passage.

Remember that it is perfectly acceptable to use either American or British English words, but it is better not to mix them up. The American English words have been included so that you will be able to recognise them in the future.

US		GB
a) highway	i)	caravan
b) hood	ii)	road surface
c) fender	iii)	pavement
d) gas(oline)	iv)	motorway
e) trunk	v)	lorry
f) trailer	vi)	toll motorway
g) pavement	vii)	boot
h) turnpike	viii)	bonnet
i) sidewalk	ix)	wing
j) truck	x)	petrol

4 Some words are spelt differently in American English. Do you know how you would spell the following in British English?
   a) tires
   b) carburetor

Reading for specific information

1 What advice would you give to the following people?

I drive to work every day in downtown Manhattan. The roads are in a bad state, and in winter are often covered with snow. Any ideas on how to reduce gas consumption?

I have to move from Houston, Texas to Vancouver in Canada. The trip will take me across the desert and the Rocky Mountains. I've got a VW Beetle without air conditioning, so it doesn't use much gas. But I still need to be as economical as possible. What do you suggest?

As I drive about 10,000 miles a year, I'm fairly fuel conscious, and I know all about driving at a steady speed, avoiding streets with potholes and heavy traffic, etc. Is there anything I can do to keep my car in good condition even before I drive off in the morning?

2 Read the passage through again and note down any information which you didn't know before.

≫→

3 Now working in pairs, try and answer this quiz. The answers are below.

ARE YOU A MILEAGE WASTER?

Pick the most fuel-efficient solutions (*see answers below*).

1. Best gas mileage is obtained if tires are...
(a) Overinflated by 3-4 pounds.
(b) Underinflated by 3-4 pounds.
(c) Inflated to manufacturer's recommended pressure.

2. You drive about 15,000 miles a year, most of it on freeways. Your subcompact gets 24 mpg, so you figure it's no big deal to cruise at 70 mph rather than the legal 55. With gas at $1.25 a gallon, how much extra will your indulgent attitude cost you annually?
(a) $95; (b) $165; (c) $235.

3. When you start the engine in the morning, do you...
(a) Let it warm up for a few minutes? (b) Apply light pressure to the accelerator while in neutral to speed warm-up? (c) Move immediately and drive slowly during the warm-up period?

4. The use of synthetic rather than regular oil...
(a) Decreases gas mileage. (b) Increases gas mileage. (c) Has no effect on mileage.

5. When you're waiting in a drive-in line, you...
(a) Turn off the engine if you must wait over 30 seconds. (b) Allow the engine to idle. (c) Try to keep the car in a level spot.

6. You do a lot of driving under severe conditions. How often should your engine have a major tuneup?
(a) With every oil change. (b) 6,000 miles or six months. (c) 12,000 miles or 12 months.

Answers to quiz: 1b, 2c, 3b, 4c, 5b, 6a.

Further work

1 Here are some tables to help you convert imperial measurements into metric.

Miles	Kilometres
5	8
10	16
25	40

Miles/gallon	Litres/100km
20	14.1
30	9.4
40	7.1

Feet	Metres
1000	305
1	0.305

Pounds/sq.in.	Kg/sq. cm
18	2.74
20	2.81
25	3.02

Work in pairs, and draw up a list of questions you would like to ask other groups to find out about the kind of driving they do. Think about mileage per year, whether it is town or country, the state of the roads they usually use, the type of car they drive etc. When you're ready, ask the other students your questions. Choose one or two of the students and draw up a chart like the one below giving advice on how to save petrol.

HOW TO SAVE PETROL

	should	should not
student A		
student B		

2 Write the answers to the letters on page 117. Try and use ten to fifteen words and expressions from this unit.

Unit 27   The Trans-Siberian Express

Predicting

1 This passage is taken from *One's Company* by Peter Fleming, and is part of his account of a journey he made on the Trans-Siberian Express in 1933. Before you read it, write down ten words which you expect to find in a passage about a train journey.
   Discuss your list of words with another student.

2 In fact, the journey on the Trans-Siberian Express takes about eight days and the train is approaching its destination. How do you expect the writer to be feeling at this stage?

3 The passage begins as the writer is suddenly woken up with a jolt and a crashing noise. Now read on.

I sat up in my berth. From the rack high above me my heaviest suitcase, metal-bound, was cannonaded down, catching me with fearful force on either knee-cap. I was somehow not particularly surprised. This is the end of the world, I thought, and in addition they have broken both   5
my legs. I had a vague sense of injustice.
   My little world was tilted drunkenly. The window showed me nothing except a few square yards of goodish grazing, of which it offered an oblique bird's-eye view. Larks were singing somewhere. It was six o'clock. I began to dress. I   10
now felt very much annoyed.
   But I climbed out of the carriage into a refreshingly spectacular world, and the annoyance passed. The Trans-Siberian Express sprawled foolishly down the embankment. The mail-van and the dining-car, which had been in front,   15
lay on their sides at the bottom. Behind them the five sleeping-cars, headed by my own, were disposed in attitudes which became less and less grotesque until you got to the last, which had remained, primly, on the rails. Fifty yards down the line the engine, which had parted company with   20
the train, was dug in, snorting, on top of the embankment. It

had a truculent and naughty look; it was defiantly conscious of indiscretion.

It would be difficult to imagine a nicer sort of railway accident. The weather was ideal. No one was badly hurt. 25 And the whole thing was done in just the right Drury Lane manner, with lots of twisted steel and splintered woodwork and turf scarred deeply with demoniac force. For once the Russians had carried something off.

The staff of the train were scattered about the wreckage, 30 writing contradictory reports with trembling hands. A charming German consul and his family– the only other foreigners on the train – had been in the last coach and were unscathed. Their small daughter, aged six, was delighted with the whole affair, which she regarded as having been 35 arranged specially for her entertainment; I am afraid she will grow up to expect too much from trains.

But it had been great fun: a comical and violent climax to an interlude in which comedy and violence had been altogether too lacking for my tastes. It was good to lie back in 40 the long grass on a little knoll and meditate upon that sprawling scrap-heap. There she lay, in the middle of a wide green plain: the crack train, the Trans-Siberian Luxury Express. For more than a week she had bullied us. She had knocked us about when we tried to clean our teeth, she had 45 jogged our elbows when we wrote, and when we read she made the print dance tiresomely before our eyes. Her whistle had arbitrarily curtailed our frenzied excursions on the wayside platforms. Her windows we might not open on account of the dust, and when closed they had proved a 50 perpetual attraction to small boys with stones. She had annoyed us in a hundred little ways: by spilling tea in our laps, by running out of butter, by regulating her life in accordance with Moscow time, now six hours behind the sun. She had been our prison. We had not liked her. 55

(Peter Fleming: *One's Company*)

4 Did the words you predicted in 1 appear in the passage?

Inferring

Work in pairs and discuss what the writer is implying by the following extracts from the passage.

a) 'I had a vague sense of injustice.' (line 6)
b) 'I now felt very much annoyed.' (lines 10–11)
c) 'For once, the Russians had carried something off.' (lines 28–9)
d) 'The staff of the train were . . . writing contradictory reports.' (lines 30–1)
e) 'I am afraid she will grow up to expect too much from trains.' (lines 36–7)
f) '. . .a comical and violent climax to an interlude in which comedy and violence had been altogether too lacking for my tastes.' (lines 38–40)

Dealing with unfamiliar words

Choose the best answer.

a) 'was cannonaded down' (line 2): (i) was broken down, (ii) had been thrown down with great force, (iii) had fallen with a resounding crash
   Clue: Think about where the suitcase had been and what it was like.
b) 'sprawled' (line 14): (i) lay in disorder, (ii) lay on its side, (iii) lay upside down
   Clue: What had happened to the mail van and to the last sleeping car?
c) 'snorting' (line 21): (i) blowing its whistle, (ii) burning vigorously, (iii) puffing steam noisily
   Clue: Think about the type of engine a train would have in 1933.
d) 'splintered' (line 27): (i) burnt, (ii) broken into small pieces, (iii) cut
   Clue: Imagine the scene. What might have happened to anything made of wood?
e) 'unscathed' (line 34): (i) ungrateful, (ii) unfriendly, (iii) unhurt
   Clue: Remember how the little girl was feeling at the time.
f) 'crack' (line 43): (i) run down, (ii) defective, (iii) first rate
   Clue: What was the reputation of the train meant to be?
g) 'bullied' (line 44): (i) attached, (ii) tormented, (iii) amused
   Clue: Had the writer had a pleasant or an unpleasant journey?

Understanding writer's style

1 One feature of the writer's style in this passage is the way in which he uses certain words and expressions which turn the train into a living and mischievous being.
   For example: 'It had a truculent and naughty look; it was defiantly conscious of indiscretion.' (lines 21–3)
   Can you find any other examples of this feature?

2 The writer also creates a humorous effect by using some elaborate expressions or constructions which could be expressed more simply.

For example: '. . .the five sleeping-cars . . . were disposed in attitudes which became less and less grotesque until you got to the last. . .' (lines 16–19)

could be rewritten: The first sleeping-car was on its side, the last one on the rails and the others in a position in between.

Re-write the following sentences.
a) '. . .the engine which had parted company with the train. . .' (lines 20–1)
b) 'Her whistle had arbitrarily curtailed our frenzied excursions on the wayside platforms.' (lines 47–9)
c) 'Her windows . . . had proved a perpetual attraction to small boys with stones.' (lines 49–51)

3 The following questions deal with some specific features of the writer's style.

a) What is the effect of the short sentences in lines 10–11?
b) Why does the writer describe the Trans-Siberian Express as sprawling 'foolishly' down the embankment? (line 14)
c) Why is the last sleeping-car described as remaining 'primly' on the rails? (lines 18–19)
d) Drury Lane is a street in the centre of London's theatre district. Why does the writer say 'And the whole thing was done in just the right Drury Lane manner. . .'? (lines 26–7)
e) What is the effect of writing 'There she lay, in the middle of a wide green plain: the *crack* train, the Trans-Siberian Luxury Express.'? (lines 42–4)

Further work

1 Towards the end of the chapter from which this passage was taken, we learn that the writer crossed the border into China and 'The train drew up in a station . . . patrolled by substantial little soldiers in grey uniforms. . . We had reached Manchuli at last.'

   Write a paragraph or two describing what happened between the train crash and the arrival in Manchuli.

2 Look through this passage again and if you have read them, the passages in units 25 and 26. Note down twenty or more words and expressions which you have learnt. Using as much of this new vocabulary as possible, write a paragraph or two on one of the following subjects:

   – What is your favourite way to travel? Explain why.
   – Describe a long distance journey you have made.
   – What is the best – and the worst – form of transport in your town?

Unit 28 On show

Understanding text organisation

1 The following sentences are taken from four brochures of exhibitions or art collections in London, listed below. Working with another student, separate the four texts and match them with the brochure titles.

National Portrait Gallery

Paintings from the Royal Academy,
   Royal Academy of Arts

English Romanesque Art 1066–1200
   Hayward Gallery

The Genius of Venice 1500–1600
   Royal Academy of Arts

a) Between November 1983 and March 1984, the Royal Academy of Arts will be mounting the greatest exhibition of Italian Old Master paintings seen in this country since the Italian exhibition of 1930, also at the Royal Academy.

b) This exhibition is about the art and architecture of Norman England in the period following the victory of William the Conqueror in 1066.

c) The National Portrait Gallery was founded in 1856, with the aim of collecting the likenesses of famous British men and women.

d) The Conquest transformed the social and political life of England and stimulated a flowering of artistic creativity which produced great secular and ecclesiastical buildings and the wealth of objects and decorations they contained.

e) The portrait provides the most vivid and tangible link between ourselves and the great personalities of the past.

f) Great or mundane, the portraits in the Gallery constitute the most comprehensive portrait survey of historical personalities to be found anywhere in the world.

g) For the past fifteen months a collection of forty important works from the Royal Academy of Arts has been on tour of the United States.

h) It will be the most valuable collection of Renaissance works of art assembled in the last fifty years and, through paintings, sculpture, prints and drawings, the exhibition will for the first time give a complete overview of Venice's Golden Age.

i) During these months some 200,000 Americans, visiting museums as widespread as New York, Seattle, New Orleans and San Antonio, have had an opportunity to learn something of the history and character of Britain's Royal Academy.

j) Here for the first time some of the great treasures of Norman England will be gathered together: sculpture, ivories, manuscripts, metalwork and stained glass.

k) The architecture of the period will be portrayed in an audio-visual display which will include such great buildings as Canterbury, Durham and Winchester Cathedrals and the Tower of London.

l) Some 200 paintings and sculptures have been assembled from throughout the world – from all the major museums as well as from the churches, galleries and private collections of Italy.

m) The paintings have been acquired by the Royal Academy over the years in a number of ways, among which the most unusual and most important is by means of newly elected Academicians, who are required to give an example of their work to the institution.

n) The primary collection at present numbers about seven thousand items. The two standards of admission are the importance of the sitter, and the authenticity of the portrait as a contemporary likeness.

o) Several have been restored specifically for the exhibition, and some have never been seen in public before.

p) The Gallery acquires about eighty new portraits a year, about half by bequest or gift, the rest by purchase.

q) Turner gave an atmospheric painting of Dolbadern Castle – a good example of his early work, for he was still in his twenties when elected.

r) A section of the exhibition will be devoted to the 17th, 18th and 19th century study of the Romanesque, including works by Turner and Cotman.

(Arts Council, National Portrait Gallery, Royal Academy)

2 Decide whether the passages describe *permanent* or *temporary* exhibitions.

Inferring

Working in pairs decide what evidence there is in the passage for the following statements. If there is no evidence or they are false, explain what the passage really says.

a) The Italian exhibition of 1930 was the first time the Italian masters had been seen in Britain.

Example: a) No evidence; the passage says that the 1930 exhibition was the last great exhibition of Italian masters.

b) The Norman Conquest took place in 1066.
c) The National Portrait Gallery has portraits of both important and unimportant people.
d) The main period of the Renaissance was the sixteenth century.
e) Certain buildings are included among the treasures of Norman England.
f) The National Portrait Gallery's collection is growing all the time.
g) The Royal Academy acquires its paintings by bequest or gift.
h) The Venice exhibition has the same selection of paintings as was seen in 1930.
i) Turner and Cotman were both Academicians.
j) The exhibition on English Romanesque Art also includes works by later artists.

Dealing with unfamiliar words

1 Write down all the words which mean different types of works of art.

2 Discuss with another student the answers to the following questions.
  a) 'secular and ecclesiastical' (sentence d): Ecclesiastical buildings are church buildings. Can you find some examples of ecclesiastical architecture referred to in the passage? What do you think secular buildings are? Can you find an example?
  b) 'vivid and tangible' (sentence e): Are these likely to be (i) positive, (ii) negative qualities of the 'link between ourselves and. . .'?
  c) 'comprehensive' (sentence f): Is this likely to be a (i) large, (ii) small portrait survey?
  d) 'widespread' (sentence i): Look at the two words which make up this word. Is it likely to mean (i) far apart, (ii) close by?
  e) 'portrayed' (sentence k): Find the noun made from this word elsewhere in the passage. Think of a word which means the same.
  f) 'sitter' (sentence n): This refers to (i) the painter, (ii) the subject of the painting.
  g) 'bequest' (sentence p): Is a bequest like (i) a gift, (ii) a purchase?

Understanding complex sentences

Certain sentences in the passage are made more complex because a participle replaces a complete relative clause. In such cases, it is difficult to decide (i) what the subject of the participle is, (ii) what the tense of the relative clause might be. Look at the following sentences and answer the questions:

a) 'Between November 1983 and March 1984. . .' (sentence a)
   i)   What is the subject of 'seen'?
   ii) The tense in the relative clause would be: which has seen.
                                                 which was seen.
                                                 which has been seen.
                                                 which will be seen.

b) 'This exhibition is about. . .' (sentence b)
   i)   What is the subject of 'following'?
   ii) The tense in the relative clause would be: which followed.
                                                 who follows.
                                                 which has followed.
                                                 who had followed.

c) 'It will be the most valuable collection. . .' (sentence h)
   i)   What is the subject of 'assembled'?
   ii) The tense of the relative clause would be: which will be assembled.
                                                 which has been assembled.
                                                 which will assemble.
                                                 which has assembled.

d) 'During these months. . .' (sentence i)
   i)   What is the subject of 'visiting'?
   ii) The tense in the relative clause would be: who has visited.
                                                 which visited.
                                                 who have visited.
                                                 which have been visiting.

e) 'A section of the exhibition. . .' (sentence r)
   i)   What is the subject of 'including'?
   ii) The tense of the relative clause would be: which is including.
                                                 which are including.
                                                 who will be included.
                                                 which includes.

Writing summaries

1 In 1984, an exhibition of Pre-Raphaelite paintings was held at the Tate Gallery in London. The Pre-Raphaelites were a group of English painters who painted in the middle years of the nineteenth century.

Look at the following notes made about the exhibition, and decide which information would be included in a short paragraph *similar in style* to the passages in this unit. Make sure you leave out any information which is not necessary for this kind of brochure.

– Vital years of Pre-Raphaelite painting: 1848–60.
– After 1860, new direction to movement.
– Sponsored by Pearson.
– Fully illustrated catalogue.
– In mid 1840s, future leaders of the movement were at the Royal Academy Schools.
– In recent years, excellent one-man shows of Pre-Raphaelite painters.
– Full range of painting is represented:
• 'hard-edge' style of Millais' early work.
• seriousness of Rossetti and Burne-Jones.

– Exhibition at the Tate Gallery.
– Paintings, drawings, sculptures.
– Open from 10 a.m. – 7 p.m every day.
– 250 works from all over the world.
– Alan Bowness, Director of Tate.
– Most comprehensive exhibition ever mounted.
– Catalogue published by Penguin.
– First comprehensive overview.
– Rossetti: most influential after 1860s.

2 Join the notes you have chosen into a short paragraph of about 100–120 words.

Further work

Work in groups of two or three, and find out what interesting exhibitions or events are worth seeing in your town at the moment. Choose one and prepare a short 'brochure' about it, explaining why it is worth seeing. Try and use at least ten words or expressions from the passage in this unit.

National Portrait Gallery

St Martin's Place
London WC2H 0HE
01-930 1552

1066
ENGLISH ROMANESQUE ART 1066-1200

THE GENIUS OF
VENICE
1500-1600

HAYWARD GALLERY,
SOUTH BANK, LONDON SE1
5 APRIL – 8 JULY 1984

AN ARTS COUNCIL EXHIBITION

PAINTINGS
FROM THE
YAL ACADEMY

return from the successful tour
of the United States

25 November 1983 – 11 March 1984
Royal Academy of Arts
Burlington House, Piccadilly, London W1

Royal Academy of Arts
Piccadilly, London W1
15 June-15 July, 1984

Admission free, through the support of BAT INDUSTRIES

Unit 29 Indiana Jones and the Temple of Doom

The passages in this unit are all reviews of the film *Indiana Jones and the Temple of Doom*.

Predicting

1 Before you read the passages, decide which of the following words you would expect to find, and in what sort of context. If you don't understand all the words, check their meaning in a dictionary.

villain	archaeologist	script
plot	adventure	cult
comic-book	craft	cheek
master	fantasy	action
goddess	hero	climax

2 Now read the passages and check whether the words you chose appear or not.

1 IN *Raiders of the Lost Ark*, the producer George Lucas and director Steven Spielberg set out to create a movie of endless climaxes to match memories of
5 the adventure serials of their youth – or, more correctly, their parents' youth before the war. Originality was to be avoided and clichés embraced with the warmth reserved for long-lost
10 friends.

It is, however, already looking tired in the sequel, **Indiana Jones and the Temple of Doom**, which again features Harrison Ford as the archaeolo-
15 gist hero.

The picture begins in 1935 Shanghai pitting 'Indy' Jones against an Oriental villain in a night-spot called the Club Obi Wan, where the resident cho-
20 reographer has the style and budget of Busby Berkeley.

'Indy', his devoted Chinese boy assistant and a belly-aching American blonde beauty (Kate Capshaw) bale out of their doomed aircraft in an in-
25 flatable rubber dinghy that does service as a parachute, a toboggan to slide down Himalayan slopes, and finally a craft to shoot the rapids in. This is 007-stuff, and, as in the Bond movies we
30 are invited to admire the producers' cheek, not compelled to share the characters' danger.

In India the trio are asked by some downtrodden villagers to rescue
35 their abducted children and retrieve a sacred stone from a sect of mad zealots who have revived the ancient cult of Thuggee under the leadership of an Oxford-educated fanatic. This,
40 the main body of the film, features extensive scenes of torture and mutilation.

Indiana Jones is a thin, graceless

45 affair. And I'm not at all sure that you can imitate pre-war imperial adventure pictures of this kind without taking a more critical or ironic attitude towards their xenophobia and sexism than Lucas and Spielberg do. 50

---

2 IN **Indiana Jones and the Temple of Doom**, Spielberg does not simply photograph the action, he makes his camera part of it, bringing the spec-
55 tator in as a fourth adventurer along with Indiana, his girl, Willie, and his sidekick, Short Round. In perfecting this technique Spielberg has borrowed the craft of the cliff-hanger serials
60 that were his role-model and turned it into a considerable art.

The script by Willard Huyck and Gloria Katz does not quite match up to the wit and verve of Lawrence
65 Kasdan's writing in *Raiders of the Lost Ark*, and lacks a certain dynamism in the middle by lingering too long in the temple, and the plight of the Indian children who have become
70 slaves of an evil maharajah is handled somewhat insensitively.

Of course, like *Raiders*, this is a comic-book fantasy ostensibly about the search for a sacred stone but really
75 just a series of cues for a dance, a spectacular drop from a plane and chase after chase after chase. Harrison Ford, repeating his role as the improbable archaeologist, looks a little more world-weary than he 80 should since the action in this film predates his more vigorous presence in *Raiders*. But his passage is enlivened by a comically wry Kate Capshaw and the young actor, Ke Huy Quan. 85

Take the scene where Indiana nearly meets his maker in a classic rope bridge conundrum: enemies on either side, hero in the middle, alligators 3,000 feet below. The master 90 shot was probably done by the director in Sri Lanka, the snarling shots of the alligators might have been left to the second unit director, maybe in another country, the close-up of Ford 95 would have been done in front of blue backing in Elstree, London and the rest of the cliff, filled in back in California by George Lucas who thought up the whole idea. 100

---

3 For background Spielberg and his associates have read enough Indian history to fill a picture postcard. The landed peasants,
105 locked into drought, starvation and exploitation, are the underdogs and therefore the good guys. The Maharajahs, with assistance from the British Raj and their own
110 corrupt politicians, are the villains. The Thuggee cult with its blood-thirsty worship of the goddess Kali, is the catalyst for the non-stop action that climaxes in the
115 ornate subterranean temple of doom.

He may be a less wholesome hero than Superman, but he comes from the same stable. Second time round, he is accompanied through 120 jungles infested with snakes, along corridors lined with leeches and through deadly spike chambers by Spielberg's giggly blonde girlfriend, Kate Capshaw and a 125 12-year-old boy of Eastern origin called Short Round.

To ram the point home here, Jones's main adversary is a diminutive totalitarian ruler who 130 threatens to upset the archaeologist's act by sticking pins into his Indy doll. With all this going for it, how can the latest Spielberg film fail? Indeed, you'd 135 better stop reading now and join the queues around the block.

(*The Sunday Times, Ms London, The Observer*)

Understanding text organisation

In each passage the first sentence of *two* of the paragraphs is missing. Read the passages and decide where the sentences below should go.

a) Nice to know, though, that not everything in this film is perfection, otherwise the director would have no new goals to aspire to.

b) The formula worked well enough in a mindless way.

c) But the unsung heroes of this exercise linger anonymously in the credits.

d) Once again Harrison Ford wears the battered hat of the archaeologist who pounds to the rescue, exuding truth, justice and the American way.

e) The scene then shifts, by way of a flight across China to the India of the Raj.

f) Our director hasn't forgotten *ET*'s child power and will never again, one suspects, make a film without a pre-teen scene-stealer centre screen.

Dealing with unfamiliar words

There may be a number of words or expressions which you don't understand in the passage. The exercises below will help you to understand some of them, but don't worry if there are more; the passages are particularly difficult, although it's not necessary to understand everything in them.

1 Write down all the adjectives and adjectival expressions to describe the three main characters in the film. Decide whether they describe positive or negative qualities.

2 Some of the difficult words or expressions are either explained elsewhere in the passages, or can be understood from the context of the sentence in which they appear. Work with another student and choose the best answer to the questions below.

a) 'toboggan' (line 27): This is a kind of vehicle used (i) on water, (ii) on snow, (iii) in the air, (iv) on the road.
    Clue: Where do they use the toboggan in the film?

b) 'To shoot the rapids in' (line 29): This means (i) to travel in at high speed, (ii) to travel in on mountain lakes, (iii) to travel in on fast mountain streams, (iv) to use as a shelter while fighting.
Clue: Craft means boat. In the Himalayas, what would be the most dangerous (and for the film, the most exciting) conditions in which you could use a boat?

c) 'abducted' (line 36): This means (i) saved, (ii) poor, (iii) in danger, (iv) taken away by force.
Clue: What or who do they have to rescue the children from?

d) 'zealots' (line 37): This means (i) religious fanatics, (ii) priests, (iii) university graduates, (iv) lunatics.
Clue: Look at the reference to the Thugees in the third review. How would you describe them?

e) 'cliff-hanger serials' (line 59): This is a serial (i) in which each episode ends on a climax, (ii) with lots of outdoor scenes, (iii) in which the action is simply photographed.
Clue: Look at the first sentence of the first review.

f) 'wit and verve' (line 64): This means the film is (i) slow and insensitive, (ii) unoriginal and tired, (iii) lively and humorous, (iv) spectacular but improbable.
Clue: Which writer(s) does the critic prefer?

g) 'classic rope bridge conundrum' (lines 87–8): This means (i) a moment of confusion on a rope bridge in ancient Greece, (ii) a dilemma in the plot in which the hero has several choices, (iii) a familiar scene in which the hero, on a rope bridge, has to escape from danger.
Clue: Where was this scene set? What sort of choice does the hero really have?

3 a) In the first review, look for words which mean the same as:
   complaining   hatred of foreigners

   b) In the second review, look for words which mean the same as:
   assistant   fate   on the surface.

   c) In the third review, look for words or expressions which mean the same as:
   highly decorated   emphasise   enemy

4 If there are any more words which you don't understand, look carefully at the context and try and guess what they might mean. You may also understand their general sense when you have done the other exercises in this unit.

Evaluating the text

1 Decide whether each review suggests that the writer thinks the film:
   i)   will be successful.
   ii)   is good in parts.
   iii) is bad.   »»→

133

2 Look at the following sentences and answer the questions.
   a) 'In *Raiders of the Lost Ark*...' (lines 1–10)
      According to the critic, what is the 'style' of this film?
   b) 'In perfecting this technique...' (lines 56–7)
      Does the reviewer like the technique or not?
   c) 'For background Spielberg and his associates...' (lines 101–4)
      Does the reviewer think the director has read a lot of Indian history?
   Look for evidence in the reviews to justify your answers and make notes.

3 Now write down the words and expressions the reviewers use to describe the
   various features of the film shown in the chart below. Remember that not all the
   boxes can be filled in.

	action/suspense	*style of film*	*camerawork/ direction*	*script*
review 1				
review 2				
review 3				

4 Decide whether the words and expressions used are positive or negative ways of
   describing these features. Put a + or a − by each box.

Writing summaries

1 Look at the reviews again and note down all the details about the plot. Compare
   your notes with another student.

2 Now working alone, put your notes in the order that the events occur in the film,
   and write a short paragraph describing the plot.

Further work

1 Find out what films, plays or other forms of entertainment the other students in
   your class have seen recently. Work with someone who has seen the same thing
   as you. Discuss what you liked and disliked about it, and whether you would
   recommend that the others should see it. Prepare a short oral or written review
   of it. Use at least ten words or expressions from the passage.
      When everyone is ready, present your review to the rest of the class.

2 Make a list of all the things which are worth seeing in your town at the moment,
   and prepare short reviews of them all for a class magazine called *What's On*.

Unit 30   An away win

Understanding text organisation

The six sections of this passage have been printed in the wrong order. Read it through and put them in the right order.

A   And the players watched, too. The game had stopped. The Mexican players kicked the turf, the Salvadorean team shouted at the Suns.
      Please return the ball. It was the announcer. He was hoarse.
      If the ball is not returned, the game will not continue.   5
      This brought a greater shower of objects from the upper seats – cups, cushions, more bottles. The bottles broke with a splashing sound on the concrete seats. The Suns lower down began throwing things back at their persecutors, and it was impossible to say where the ball had gone.   10
      The ball was not returned. The announcer repeated his threat.

B   Soon, a bad kick landed the ball into the Shades. This ball was fought for and not thrown back, and one could see the ball progressing through the section. The ball was seldom visible, but one could tell from the free-for-alls – now here, now there –   15
      where it was. The Balconies poured water on the Shades, but the ball was not surrendered. And now it was the Suns' turn to see the slightly better-off Salvadoreans in the Shades section behaving like swine. The announcer made his threat: the game would not resume until the ball was thrown back. The threat   20
      was ignored, and after a long time the ref walked onto the field with a new ball.

C   The players sat down on the field and did limbering-up exercises until, ten minutes after the ball had disappeared from the field, a new ball was thrown in. The spectators cheered but,   25
      just as quickly, fell silent. Mexico had scored another goal.

D   In all, five balls were lost this way. The fourth landed not far from where I sat, and I could see that real punches were being

thrown, real blood spurting from Salvadorean noses, and the
broken bottles and the struggle for the ball made it a contest all 30
its own, more savage than the one on the field, played out with
the kind of mindless ferocity you read about in books on gory
medieval sports. The announcer's warning was merely ritual
threat; the police did not intervene – they stayed on the field
and let the spectators settle their own scores. The players grew 35
bored: they ran in place, they did push-ups. When play resumed
and Mexico gained possession of the ball it deftly moved down
the field and invariably made a goal. But this play, these goals –
they were no more than interludes in a much bloodier sport
which, towards midnight (and the game was still not over!), was 40
varied by Suns throwing firecrackers at each other and onto the
field.

E   National anthems were played, amplified songs from
scratched records, and then the game began. It was apparent
from the outset who would win. Mexico was bigger, faster, and 45
seemed to follow a definite strategy; El Salvador had two
ball-hoggers, and the team was tiny and erratic. The crowd
hissed the Mexicans and cheered El Salvador. One of the
Salvadorean ball-hoggers went jinking down the field, shot and
missed. The ball went to the Mexicans, who tormented the 50
Salvadoreans by passing it from man to man and then, fifteen
minutes into the game, the Mexicans scored. The stadium was
silent as the Mexican players kissed one another.

F   Some minutes later the ball was kicked into the Shades
section. It was thrown back into the field and the game was 55
resumed. Then it was kicked into the Suns section. The Suns
fought for it; one man gained possession, but he was pounced
upon and the ball shot up and ten Suns went tumbling after it. A
Sun tried to run down the steps with it. He was caught and the
ball wrestled from him. A fight began, and now there were 60
scores of Suns punching their way to the ball. The Suns higher
up in the section threw bottles and cans and wadded paper on
the Suns who were fighting, and the shower of objects – meat
pies, bananas, hankies – continued to fall. The Shades, the
Balconies, the Anthill watched this struggle. 65

(Paul Theroux: *The Old Patagonian Express*)

Inferring

Decide what evidence there is in the passage for the following statements.

a) The match probably took place in El Salvador.
b) The Shades, the Suns, the Balconies and the Anthill are the names given by the writer for the different sections of the stadium.
c) The Shades were more expensive seats than the Suns.
d) After a while, the players simply waited calmly while the ball was retrieved.
e) The Balconies were above the Shades.
f) As soon as a new ball was thrown in, the Mexicans scored a goal.

Linking ideas

Write down all the words and expressions used which refer to the *football spectators*.

Writing summaries

1 Answer the following questions in note form.
a) Who was the match between?
Example: a) El Salvador and Mexico.

b) Who was likely to win?
c) When did the Mexicans first score?
d) Then what happened when the ball was kicked into the Suns?
e) What did the players do?
f) How was the match restarted?
g) What happened then?
h) How many balls were lost in all?
i) What happened when the fourth ball was kicked into the Shades?
j) What happened whenever the Mexicans gained possession of the ball?
k) What did the writer consider to be the real sport?

2 Without looking back at the passage, use your notes to write full answers to the questions above.

3 Use the sentences to write a summary of the passage; it should be about 120–150 words long. If it is longer, re-write the sentences excluding any unnecessary words or expressions. Make sure you include all the main points.

4 Re-read the passage and check that you have included all the essential points.

Further work

1 Work in groups of two or three. Make a list of all the sports which are played in your country or countries. Find out when and where they were first played. Then choose one of them and prepare a short history of the sport. Make sure you don't choose the same sport as other groups. When everyone is ready, give your presentation to the rest of the class.

2 In groups of two or three, discuss whether it is the spectator or the sport itself which arouses this kind of violent reaction.

3 Look through this passage again and, if you have read them, the passages in units 28 and 29. Note down twenty or so words and expressions which you have learnt. Using as much of the new vocabulary as possible, write a short paragraph on one of the following subjects:
   – Can we afford the 'Arts' in present day society?
   – Describe your favourite play or film.
   – 'Sport is the modern substitute for warfare.' Discuss.

Unit 31   Should the Press be human?

Predicting

This passage discusses the responsibilities of journalists in carrying out their professional duties. Before you read the passage, look at the title of this unit and discuss with another student what you think it means. Think about the following points.
a) What are the responsibilities of a journalist? Make a short list.
b) What do you think '(to) be human' means?
c) Can you think of any situations when the journalist might not be human?

Extracting main ideas

1 The title expresses the main idea of this passage. Now read the passage and decide which of the following sentences expresses the title in a more complete way. Discuss your answers with another student.

   a) 'Journalists and TV people. . .sometimes seem amazingly cold-blooded.' (lines 13–17)
   b) 'Should these journalists and photographers join in, or just stand back and watch while people kill one another?' (lines 29–31)
   c) '. . .how will the world know, how should the world believe what atrocities are committed?' (lines 34–7)
   d) 'Our professional ethic enjoins us to stay uncommitted and report the facts; and, if we have to have guidelines, that's probably as good a one as any.' (lines 41–4)

2 The title asks a question. Which of the following sentences contains the writer's reply?

   a) 'My complaint against journalists. . .is not that they behave badly in the course of duty, but their inability to recoil into a human being when it's over.' (lines 53–7)
   b) 'To stay out of the fight. . .that is supposed to be our code. . .' (lines 66–71)
   c) '. . .and when it comes to the crunch, we probably do better trying to stick to that, than rushing off on individual impulse.' (lines 71–4)
   d) 'But is there not a point in any profession. . .I think there is. . .' (lines 75–81)

140

A IF YOU were asked who shot Lee Harvey Oswald you would probably say Jack Ruby. But there's another possible answer to the question: the photographer
5 who shot those staggering pictures of Ruby gunning him down. And what has teased my mind ever since is wondering whether, if he had dropped his camera and grabbed the gunman, we might, with
10 Oswald alive, know more than we will now ever be able to find out about why Kennedy died.

B   Journalists and TV people, we know, are supposed to record what goes on; but
15 in trying to get the best record they can, they may sometimes seem amazingly cold-blooded. In the massacre that followed the British quitting India, there was a photographer who made a sorrow-
20 ing Indian family bury and rebury its dead several times till he got a perfect shot. A BBC sound man held up a Nigerian execution for half an hour while he adjusted his sound equipment; you could
25 say it didn't make any difference to the final outcome, but it doesn't make you feel especially warm towards the man concerned.

C   Should these journalists and photogra-
30 phers join in, or just stand back and watch while people kill one another? It's a tricky ethical question, not just a matter of how brave anyone is feeling at the time; because without authentic pictures, how
35 will the world know, how should the world believe what atrocities are committed? One dead photographer does not do much for the cause he cares about, even if he did feel compelled to weigh in
40 and take sides.

D   Our professional ethic enjoins us to stay uncommitted and report the facts; and, if we have to have guidelines, that's probably as good a one as any. Certainly some
45 of the seediest of journalists, whether we're talking about the Middle East or Northern Ireland, are those who pile on one set of adjectives—squalid, butchering, oppressive—for terrorism of whose

aims they disapprove, and quite another 50 set—committed, dedicated, idealistic— for the same thing done by those they like.

But it leaves out a lot. 'My complaint E against journalists,' a friend of mine once said, 'is not that they behave badly in the 55 course of duty, but their inability to recoil into a human being when it's over.' I have not forgotten an occasion over 20 years ago, when a birdman was going to jump from a Press-filled Rapide. He got his 60 equipment tangled with the aeroplane in some way, and plunged to his death. As most of them watched in shocked horror, one newsman ran down the plane with the words: 'My God, what a story!' 65

To stay out of the fight, to write down F what's going on, to treat equally with both sides, as a doctor will stitch up soldiers in either uniform or a lawyer argue for either side—that is supposed to be our 70 code; and when it comes to the crunch, we probably do better trying to stick to that, than rushing off on individual impulse.

But is there not a point in any profession G 75 where you are forced back against the wall as a human being, where a doctor should hand Jack the Ripper over to the police and a lawyer refuse to suppress the bloodstained evidence that proves his client a 80 torturer? I think there is, and I was heartened as well as relieved by one story told in Edward Behr's book, 'Anybody Here Been Raped & Speaks English?' During the Algerian confusion, some 85 Tunisian soldiers were preparing to shoot their prisoners ('what a story'). One journalist, an Italian, walked over and just calmly stood in front of the wretched men, implying that if the soldiers shot 90 them, they would have to shoot him too. Finally some officers arrived and defused the explosive situation, and just a handful of the lives that went up in that particular bonfire were saved. 95

A newshound may start out just to get a H good story, but it is not impossible, all the same, for him to end as a man.

(Katharine Whitehorn in *The Observer*)

Dealing with unfamiliar words

1 Look through the passage again and note down all the words which describe people who work in journalism in some form or other.

2 If you don't understand the exact meaning of the words below, try and guess their general sense from the context. Choose the most likely answer.

   a) 'staggering' (line 5): This means something like (i) astonishing, (ii) exciting, (iii) badly focussed.
   b) 'cold-blooded' (line 17): This means something like (i) calm, (ii) brutal, (iii) lacking in feeling.
   c) 'atrocities' (line 36): These are likely to be acts of (i) cruelty, (ii) war (iii) kindness.
   d) 'enjoins' (line 41): This means something like (i) encourages (ii) discourages.
   e) 'seediest' (line 45): This is likely to mean (i) the best (ii) the worst, (iii) the most cold-blooded.
   f) 'squalid, butchering, oppressive' (line 48): These words are likely to have (i) positive, (ii) negative connotations.
   g) 'committed, dedicated, idealistic' (line 51): These words are likely to have (i) positive, (ii) negative connotations.
   h) 'suppress' (line 79): This means something like (i) to prevent something from being seen, (ii) to allow something to be seen.
   i) 'defused' (line 92): In this context, it means that the officers (i) reduced the tension, (ii) increased the tension in the situation.

3 There may still be some other words which you don't understand. Try writing down the whole sentence in which they appear, but excluding the difficult word itself. See if you can understand the general sense of the sentence without being distracted by the word.

Understanding text organisation

1 As you saw in 1 of *Extracting main ideas*, the writer presents the two options facing a journalist:
   X – Should these journalists and photographers join in?
   or Y – (Should they) just stand back and watch while people kill each other?
   Look at the passage again and discuss with another student which option each paragraph refers to. Write the number of the paragraph and X or Y according to the option.

2 Now decide which sentences express the argument explaining the *options*, and which sentences illustrate the argument with *examples*. Write down the line

numbers of the sentences in the chart below. The first one has been done for you.

argument	example
lines 13-17	lines 1-12

3 Which of the sentences in the argument column express both options? By each line reference, write down X, Y or X + Y.

Writing summaries

1 In *Understanding text organisation*, you saw that the passage consists of the two options facing the journalist, with the arguments and examples supporting both sides of the dilemma. Most summaries require you to express the main ideas of a passage in about 120–150 words, so you may not have room to include many examples here.
   a) Without looking back at the passage, make notes on the two options.
   b) Then write notes on the argument supporting one option.
   c) Next, write notes on the argument supporting the other option.
   d) Finally, write notes on what you think the writer's conclusion is.
   Now read the passage again and check that you have accurately expressed the general sense of the passage.

2 Now join your notes together in connected sentences. Begin each section with the following phrases:
   a) The author asks the question. . .   c) On the other hand. . .
   b) On the one hand. . .   d) The writer's conclusion is that. . .

3 Read the passage again and make sure you have left nothing out. Check that you haven't written more than 150 words.

Further work

1 Work in groups of two or three. Look at some newspapers and choose an article and/or a photograph on a matter of social or human importance. Decide whether there was anything the journalist might have been able to do to help or prevent the situation which is being described. Discuss your ideas with the rest of the class.

2 The writer talks about how journalists sometimes give a biased view of the news according to their own opinions of the matter. Choose a news report and re-write it from a completely different viewpoint. For example, you may like to choose a report of a burglary and re-write it from the point of view of the burglar.

Unit 32   Pregnant Di still wants divorce!

Extracting main ideas

1 Read the passage and fill in the blanks (1–4) with suitable headlines chosen from
the list on page 146.

LEAF THROUGH some foreign
newspapers and magazines and there
is an abundance of fascinating stories.
All about a family which, at first
5 glance, seems rather familiar.

There's Elizabeth and Philip,
Charles and Diana, Anne and Mark,
Andrew, Edward and a youngster
called William. Friends are called
10 Koo and Katie.

Yet it's very perplexing . . . the
stories don't seem to relate to the
Royal Family we think we know.

The other Diana, for example, is
15 seeking a divorce. Charles, it seems,
". . . feels like the loneliest man in
the world". And how about this
corker of a story, carried by an
American paper, the *Globe*, that a
20 royal gardener is the 'real' father of
Di's baby!"

More of which later . . .

The stories are all "authenticated"
by quotes from a huge band of "royal
25 observers", "close friends" and
"Palace insiders". Certainly . . . the
tales are a tribute to the incredible
imagination of overseas hacks.

In March, the *Globe* ran the sen-
30 sational headline: **1**
with the whispered
subheading: "Tells Queen: 'I'll take
the children with me'". Reading on,
we learnt: "Princess Diana —still
35 determined to leave Prince Charles
despite her new pregnancy—is now
locked in a bitter, secret battle over
the custody of little Prince William

and her unborn child.

"Di has told her closest friends she 40
feels Charles humiliated her by insist-
ing on a trial separation even after she
had broken the news to him that she
was expecting their second baby."

No matter that the "trial separation" 45
was Charles' trip to Africa. Diana is
apparently unappeased and she has
given the Queen a 12-month deadline
to approve the divorce.

"It's all so tragic and unnecessary," 50
another Palace insider says in the
Globe. "Charles and Diana are like
two spoiled children who need their
heads banged together."

Well, quite. On the other hand, it 55
all depends which paper you read.
For according to another American
paper, the *National Enquirer*, all is
harmony at Highgrove. And if Diana
does get a bit tense, well . . . "She 60
wears a very sexy leotard, switches on
the stereo and just lets rip!" a "former
servant" reveals.

The *Star* in America—in the same
stable as Britain's *The Sun*— which 65
sent photographers crawling through
tropical undergrowth for pics of Diana
in a bikini—is a contender for the
longest-headline-of-the-year award.

2
Phew! If you had 70
the energy to continue, you would
learn that it was the skiing holiday in
Liechtenstein and a spell away from
royal pressures which led to Charles'
and Diana's happy announcement of 75

144

a second pregnancy.

"As one royal insider put it: 'Their marriage was not all it appeared to be on the surface. The easy-going
80 Charles actually admitted to a friend only recently: 'Sometimes I feel like the loneliest man in the world. The age gap is overwhelming. William is our only common meeting ground.'"

85 Even then, if you believe what you read, they hardly ever see the poor mite anyway. Under the shock-horror headline: **3**

comes the story:
90 "Royal insiders are reeling in shock because Princess Diana and Prince Charles are said to have abandoned little Prince William to his American-born nanny and a royal gardener—to
95 raise as they see fit."

Di, you understand, spends most of her time shopping and posing for pictures, says the *Globe*. Charles, on the other hand, is too busy with
100 "royal duties" to lavish more than a few hours a week on the boy.

Now an "insider" has spilled the beans on how, in effect, gardener Fred Browning and Barbara Barnes
105 are the "real" parents.

"They (Charles and Diana) have no idea that William is growing up to love a lowly weed-puller and look upon him as a father figure," the
110 source says. "It's tragic because he's growing up apart from his natural parents.

"There's no doubt that he looks upon Fred and Barb as his real
115 mother and father . . . William is virtually on a love ration."

The Palace takes all the reports with a hefty pinch of salt. Michael Shea is unperturbed by these accounts.
120 "We get a large number of calls from the foreign press," he said. "Probably most come from America, France and Germany. We do get a lot of strange enquiries . . . too many to
125 document. Some are really most absurd.

"We don't have time to keep a check on all the foreign reports, but, anyway, we don't take any notice of
130 the inaccuracies. Even the most out-

landish ones we just ignore entirely."

It would probably be safe to assume though, that the proprietor of *Truth* newspaper in Australia blew his
135 chances of a knighthood when the paper published a picture of a nude girl with Princess Diana's head delicately superimposed on top.

As for the Queen, the American *National Enquirer* tapped a "source
140 close to the royal family" who revealed: "She's been walking around the Palace switching off lights . . . Even the Palace chefs were told not to throw food out— any leftovers are
145 dished up the following day. It's incredible . . ."

It certainly is. But then speculation is always rife about the Queen— especially where her health is
150 concerned.

In *Frau Aktuell*, a German magazine, new questions were asked under the headline: **4**

No matter that this report came
155 five days before her trip to Jordan. It showed pictures of other members of the Royal Family going about their duties, and then questioned: "But where is the Queen? One puzzle after
160 another has surrounded the Queen. Why does she not make any public appearances? Why does the Head of the State award public honours in Buckingham Palace where the public
165 has no access?"

The answer comes later: "Unofficially, reports have emerged that the Queen is suffering from arthritis complaints and regular attacks of
170 migraine."

At least Germany has a reason for their interest. Gerd Treuhaft, correspondent for a variety of German magazines, explains: "Not having
175 royalty, countries like France and Germany give royal stories priority. Whatever they do, it's a news item. And, don't forget, many of the British royals have German blood . . ."
180

But some royal accounts from the world's press are less amusing. Such an account appeared in the *Globe*, saying: "Diana is desperately afraid

»»→

185 to make new friends as she believes she is a deadly jinx on the people closest to her.

"She is convinced that Princess Grace is the latest victim of the 190 tragedies that have stalked her since childhood."

The deaths of President Sadat, Lord Mountbatten and Princess Grace are all listed as evidence.

195 "A close friend of Diana's told the *Globe*, 'Diana just cried and cried when Grace died . . . she started to say that she was responsible and that trouble followed her wherever she 200 went.'"

Cliff Barr, editor of the *Globe*, said: "We get stories from Palace sources and although we don't identify them, we are satisfied that they are in a position to be aware of what's going 205 on."

"The person we're all interested in is Diana. We probably run a story on Diana on page one about once every three weeks." 210

"People in England file the stories. I think our readers believe them. We do."

"A few exiled Britons take exception to some of the stories, in the way 215 they did when they belatedly found out about Edward and Mrs Simpson. They dismissed the rumours as hogwash. As far as we're concerned, the stories we print are the truth." 220

(Suzanne Thomas in *Woman*)

a) HOW THE QUEEN HELPED DI BEAT MARITAL STRESS TO FIND JOY OVER BABY SHE DESPERATELY WANTED

b) THE REAL FATHER OF DI'S BABY

c) THE PRINCESS DI NOBODY KNOWS

d) PREGNANT DI STILL WANTS DIVORCE

e) HOW QUEEN ELIZABETH SPENDS $5.4 MILLION A YEAR . . . AND WHY SHE NEEDS MORE

f) DI FEARS THE CURSE THAT'S KILLED FIVE FRIENDS

g) PUZZLE SURROUNDING THE QUEEN? IS AN ILLNESS CAUSING HER PUBLIC SHYNESS?

Check your answers with another student.

2 In the passage there are three other 'reports' about the Royal Family. Find the lines in the text which correspond to the remaining headlines on the list.

3 Do you think the writer of the passage believes all these reports? Look for evidence to justify your answer.

4 In two cases the writer gives explanations for the 'reports'. Which are they?

Dealing with unfamiliar words

There are a number of idiomatic or slang words and expressions in the passage which you may find difficult to understand. Match the words from the passage on the left with their probable meanings in the column on the right.

a) 'leaf' (line 1)
b) 'corker of a story' (line 18)
c) 'hacks' (line 28)
d) 'lets rip' (line 62)
e) 'pics' (line 67)
f) 'mite' (line 87)
g) 'spilled the beans' (lines 102–3)
h) 'weed-puller' (line 108)
i) 'takes. . .with a pinch of salt' (lines 117–18)
j) 'hogwash' (line 218)

i) dances wildly
ii) told the full story
iii) astonishing report
iv) child
v) nonsense
vi) journalists
vii) doubts whether they are true
viii) look
ix) photographs
x) gardener

Linking ideas

Write down all the words and expressions used to refer to *representatives of the Press* and *Palace insider(s)*.

Inferring

Work with another student. What evidence is there in the passage for the following statements? If there is no evidence, explain what the passage really says.

a) The writer of the article thinks that there are two separate Royal Families.
b) The writer doesn't believe any of the reports written about the Royal Family which are quoted here.
c) According to the writer, Charles' trip to Africa wasn't a trial separation.
d) The writer doesn't consider the *Star* in America or *The Sun* in Britain to be reputable newspapers.
e) The writer doesn't think Charles and Diana see much of their son.
f) The writer believes Di spends most of her time shopping and posing for pictures.
g) Michael Shea works for the Royal Family.
h) According to one report, the Queen is trying to save money.
i) According to another report, the Queen was too ill to go to Jordan.
j) According to the editor of the *Globe*, the stories are true because they come from authentic sources.

Evaluating the text

It is sometimes difficult in this passage to decide exactly who is writing certain sentences. Decide *who* wrote the following extracts. Choose from (i) the writer of the passage, (ii) a newspaper journalist, (iii) Michael Shea, the Palace spokesman.

a) 'And how about this corker of a story. . .' (lines 17–22)
b) 'No matter that the trial separation. . .' (lines 45–6)
c) 'As one royal insider put it. . .' (lines 77–9)
d) 'We don't have time to keep a check on. . .' (lines 127–31)
e) 'But then speculation has always been rife about the Queen. . .' (lines 148–51)
f) 'As far as we're concerned the stories we print are the truth.' (lines 219–20)

Further work

1 There are many newspapers which either invent reports about people and events, or attach their own misleading interpretations to facts which are otherwise quite straightforward. In groups of two or three, discuss why you think newspapers do this. Try and find examples of this kind of journalism in newspapers you know well. (The newspapers can be in your own language if necessary.) Choose two or three articles and present a short report to the rest of the class. Then organise a debate on the responsibilities of the Press towards its readers.

2 Choose a well-known person and write a 'fantastic' article about him or her for the *Globe* newspaper. Use ten to fifteen words and expressions from the passage.

Unit 33 How do you feel?

This passage is by Clive James, a television critic, and deals with the media coverage of the siege at the Iranian Embassy, London, in 1980.

Understanding text organisation

Read the passage through and fill in the gaps with the following discourse markers: *while, when, unless, but, yet, if, nor, so*. Remember that some of them can be used more than once.

WHILE the Special Air Service covered itself with glory, the viewing public gloried in the coverage. Both the BBC and ITN were there in strength
5 throughout the siege – which, for those of you with short memories, occurred at the Iranian Embassy in Knightsbridge.

The BBC gave you the front of the
10 building and ITN gave you the back. All the cameras were plugged in on a semi-permanent basis ......**1**........ their crews settled down to the daunting task of consuming the meals provided
15 for them according to the rigid specifications laid down by their unions. Days went by, then everything happened in a flash, not to mention with a bang.

20 Unfortunately for the news-gatherers most of it happened inside the building. ......**2**........ the stun grenades went off a certain amount of flame and debris emerged from the windows.
25 You could hear the bop-bop-bop of automatic weapons being fired. Afterwards there were ambulances, fire engines and a press conference.

The next group of terrorists to try

this trick will probably have the sense 30 to invite the cameras inside. The news crews, ...**3**....... the law tells them not to, will probably do their best to accept the invitation. For the terrorists, publicity is half the point. For the media, 35 a siege is just too good a story to pass up. The television news teams were drunk on adrenalin for days afterwards. ......**4**....... Constable Lock got home, he found ITN waiting for him. 'No, 40 no,' said Constable Lock politely. 'Another time maybe, but not now.' 'WHAT ARE YOU GOING TO DO WHEN YOU GET INSIDE?' 'Well, I'm going to see my children . . .' 45 'HOW DO YOU FEEL?' 'No, no. I've got to go now. Later.'

On *Newsnight* (BBC2) the BBC sound technician who had been caught up in the nightmare told his story at 50 length. As a sound technician he is not required to possess the gift of vivid speech ......**5**..... it would have been foolish to expect that the scenes he had lived through would come alive. That 55 he himself was alive, along with all the other hostages except two, was something to be grateful for. ......**6**....... I think the time has now come to be a bit sceptical about the role of television and the Press in these matters.

......**7**........ the siege is on, the media give it stature. When it is over, they help prepare the stage for the next one. The ecstatic articles about the SAS currently appearing in the newspapers are a case in point. Next time the rescue might not come off, whereupon the SAS, owing to the expectations of infallibility which have been built up, will be held to have failed.

The cold, dull truth is that when self-loading weapons are fired in confined spaces, even ......**8**........ they are being wielded by trained men firing single, aimed shots, innocent people can very easily get killed. The thing to do is to avoid sieges in the first place, not indulge in wild fantasies about camouflaged supermen licensed to wipe out wogs.

It is only in civilised countries that this kind of terrorism can hope to succeed. To leave the terrorists unpublicised would be to render them ineffective, but the terrorists are able to count on the likelihood that in a civilised country the freedom of information will not be restricted. ....**9**...........

there are many freedoms which a civilised country must restrict .....**10**....... it is to stay civilised, the classic example being the freedom to shout 'Fire!' in a crowded theatre. The time might now have come for the freedom to report certain terrorist acts to be restricted.

The problem would be one of definition, ...**11**...... need not be insuperable on that account. The present voluntary code of media conduct might, for example, be improved ......**12**..... it could be agreed that the public interest may require certain terrorist acts, involving the seizure of hostages, to be reported only after their release. Normal access to information would be allowed, ...**13**...... its dissemination would be delayed. As things stand, we can expect London to become a vast TV studio with ambitious performers heading towards it from all over the world. ......**14**..... will the prospect of being blown away by the SAS prove much of a deterrent. I have hung around television studios long enough to know that there are people perfectly ready to commit suicide in order to star in a show of their own, even when they have nothing to say.

(Clive James in *The Observer*)

Extracting main ideas

Which *two* of the following extracts summarise the main idea of the passage?

a) 'The next group of terrorists to try this trick will probably have the sense to invite the cameras inside.' (lines 29–31)
b) 'That he himself was alive, along with all the other hostages except two, was something to be grateful for.' (lines 55–8)
c) 'The time might have come for the freedom to report certain terrorist acts to be restricted.' (lines 94–7)
d) 'The present voluntary code of media conduct might, for example, be improved if it could be agreed that the public interest may require certain terrorist acts, involving the seizure of hostages, to be reported only after their release.' (lines 100–7)

Inferring

Decide what evidence there is in the passage for the following statements.
Note the writer's use of irony.

a) The writer doesn't think the media had much to do during the siege.
b) Even the end of the siege was not particularly exciting to watch.
c) The interview with the sound technician was not very interesting.
d) At the time this article was written, the SAS had a very high reputation with the general public.
e) If the SAS failed to rescue the hostages next time, it would not be their fault.
f) Terrorism succeeds in civilised countries because of the publicity it attracts.
g) The writer thinks it right that shouting 'Fire!' in a crowded theatre should be illegal.
h) The writer expects more terrorist acts of this kind in London.
i) The writer thinks people are prepared to do anything in order to appear on television.

Understanding complex sentences

This exercise focusses on the way the sentences work rather than on the writer's ironic intention.
Look at the following extracts and answer the questions.

a) 'All the cameras were plugged in. . .' (lines 11–16)
    i)   What did the crews do?
    ii) Does the passage say who provided the meals?
    iii) What was the role of the unions?

b) 'The ecstatic articles about the SAS. . .' (lines 65–7)
    i)   Who or what is appearing in the newspapers?
    ii) What does 'a case in point' refer to?

c) 'The cold dull truth is that. . .' (lines 72–7)
    i)   When are the self-loading weapons likely to be dangerous?
    ii) Is it inevitable that they should be dangerous, in these circumstances?

d) 'To leave the terrorists unpublicised. . .' (lines 84–9)
    i)   How could terrorists be deprived of their power?
    ii) What can they be sure of?

e) 'The present voluntary code of media conduct. . .' (lines 100–7)
    i)   What could be done to improve media conduct?
    ii) To what kind of terrorist acts would this proposal apply?

Writing summaries

1 Answer the following questions in *note* form. Make sure you include all the
  main ideas.

  a) What is the writer's opinion about media coverage of the siege?
  b) Why is he sceptical about the role of TV and the Press?
  c) What might happen if another siege occurs?
  d) Why are sieges likely to succeed in civilised countries?
  e) According to the writer, what should be restricted?
  f) How does he suggest that it should be restricted?
  g) What can be expected to happen if it is not restricted?

2 The notes you made in 1 are the key points which you should include in a
  summary. Without looking back at the text, use them to write full answers to the
  questions above.

3 Now join the sentences together into a single paragraph. Count the number of
  words; try not to go over 150. If there are too many, try and shorten any long
  phrases rather than exclude any of the main points. Then read the passage again
  to check you have left nothing out.

Further work

1 In fact, what the writer is suggesting in the passage is a form of censorship on
  information. Do you agree with him? Find two other students who have the
  same views as you. Note down any ideas you may have to support your
  opinions.
     Prepare notes for a short speech in which you will explain your views to the
  rest of the class. Make sure that each member of the group can talk for about
  two minutes.
     When everyone is ready, discuss with the rest of the class 'Should information
  be restricted and if so, under what circumstances?'

2 Imagine you were taken hostage. Choose ten or more words or expressions from
  the passage and write a paragraph describing what happened.

3 Look back at the passage and, if you have read them, the passages in units 31
  and 32. Note down any new words and expressions which you have learnt.
  Using as much of this new vocabulary as possible, write a paragraph or two on
  one of the following subjects:
  – Describe the political bias of the media in your country.
  – Should the news always try to be objective?

Unit 34   Childhood: pathways of discovery

Understanding text organisation

The following passage comes from a book called *Childhood: Pathways of Discovery*. The paragraphs are in the correct sequence, but the sentences in each one have been printed in the wrong order. Read the passage and put the sentences in the correct order.

Extracting main ideas

1 Look at the passage quickly and decide which of the following chapters in the book it is likely to be found in.
   a) The challenges of growth.
   b) Parent's societies and children.
   c) Knowing the world.
   d) Going to school.
   e) Who am I?
   f) Problems of development.

2 The passage discusses two contrasting views on whether children under the age of three should go to school. Decide which two of the following statements best summarise these contrasting views.

   a) If pre-school for under three year olds caused problems, it would not be so widespread.
   b) There is no negative long-term effect on infants who are sent to school before they are three years old.
   c) There is no negative effect on children who are sent to school after the age of three and a half.
   d) Traditional societies separate the child from the parent at an early age.
   e) Infants under the age of three should not be sent to nursery school.

3 Now write a sentence in your own words summarising the writer's conclusion.

Some people have drawn the conclusion from Bowlby's work that children should not be subjected to day care* before the age of three because of the parental separation it entails, and many people do believe this. But there are also arguments against such a strong conclusion. It has been argued that an 5
infant under three who is cared for outside the home may suffer because of the separation from his parents. The British psychoanalyst John Bowlby maintains that separation from the parents during the sensitive 'attachment' period from birth to three may scar a child's personality and predispose to emotional 10
problems in later life.

But traditional societies are so different from modern societies that comparisons based on just one factor are hard to interpret. Firstly anthropologists point out that the secluded love affair between children and parents found in modern 15
societies does not usually exist in traditional societies. For example, we saw earlier that among the Ngoni the father and mother of a child did not rear their infant alone – far from it.

But Bowlby's analysis raises the possibility that early day care has delayed effects. The possibility that such care might 20
lead to, say, more mental illness or crime 15 or 20 years later can only be explored by the use of statistics. Statistical studies of this kind have not yet been carried out, and even if they were, the results would be certain to be complicated and controversial. Secondly, common sense tells us that day care 25
would not be so widespread today if parents, caretakers or paediatricians found that children had problems with it. But tests that have had to be used to measure this development are not widely enough accepted to settle the issue. Thirdly, in the last decade, there have been a number of careful American 30
studies of children in day care, and they have uniformly reported that day care had a neutral or slightly positive effect on children's development.

But whatever the long-term effects, parents sometimes find the immediate effects difficult to deal with. At the age of three 35
or three and a half almost all children find the transition to nursery easy, and this is undoubtedly why more and more parents make use of child care at this time. Children under three are likely to protest at leaving their parents and show unhappiness. The matter, then, is far from clear-cut, though 40
experience and available evidence indicate that early care is reasonable for infants.

* *Note:* 'day care' means the same as 'nursery school'.

(Sheldon White, Barbara Notkin White: *Childhood: Pathways of Discovery*)

Dealing with unfamiliar words

1 Write down all the words and expressions used to describe *pre-school education*.

2 Each word on the left is related in meaning to the group of four words on the right. Choose the word on the right which is most similar in meaning to the one on the left, in the context of this passage.

a) 'maintains' (line 8)   supports   provides   argues   pretends
b) 'interpret' (line 14)   analyse   suppose   translate   define
c) 'settle' (line 29)   descent   decide   calm   pay
d) 'transition' (line 36)   move   transformation   turn   improvement
e) 'indicate' (line 41)   mean   hint   suggest   prove

3 Find words or phrases in the passage which here mean the same as:

a) involves   e) examined
b) looked after   f) common
c) damage   g) all
d) bring up   h) handle

Evaluating the text

The two sides of the argument are:
1 Infants under the age of three should not be sent to nursery school.

2 There is no negative effect on infants who are sent to school before they are three years old.
Look at the following sentences and decide which side of the argument they support.

a) 'The British psychoanalyst John Bowlby maintains that separation from the parents. . .' (lines 7–11)
b) 'For example, we saw earlier that among the Ngoni the father and mother. . .' (lines 16–18)
c) 'Secondly, common sense tells us that day care would not be so widespread today. . .' (lines 25–9)
d) 'Thirdly, in the last decade there have been. . .' (lines 29–33)
e) 'But whatever the long term effects, parents sometimes find. . .' (lines 34–5)
f) 'Children under three are likely to protest. . .and show unhappiness.' (lines 38–40)

Writing summaries

1 Using the chart below and the passage, write notes in answer to the question: 'Should children under the age of three be sent to school?'

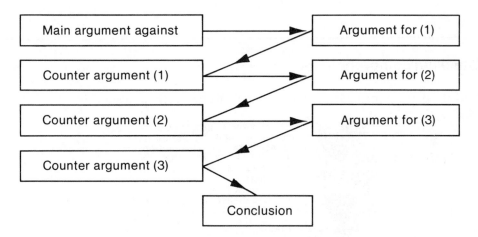

2 Now write a paragraph summarising the passage in no more than 120 words.

Further work

1 Work in groups of two or three. At what age are children obliged to go to school in your country or countries? Is there any pre-school education? If so, what kind of activities are organised for the children? What are the advantages and disadvantages of sending children to nursery school? Do you think the aims of primary school education are very different from those of pre-school education? What do you think the aims of education in general should be? Discuss your answers to these questions and present your views to the rest of the class.

2 Write a paragraph or two describing your first day at school.

Unit 35　Village voice

Checking comprehension

Read the passage through and then answer the questions opposite.

VILLAGE VOICE

Victor Zorza

A Himalayan Village

THE WOMAN had been sent
to the village by the Government, but she did not act
like an official. She humbly
5　asked permission to address
the village elders. " I've come
to help your children," she
said. " Or to take them away
10　from us," the mothers whispered, and hid their
offspring.

The elders were suspicious
too, but let her have a hut
15　— the most dilapidated in
the village. That was how to
get rid of an unwanted guest.
Leela carried her own water
from the distant well, and
20　gathered wood for the cooking. The village watched. At
first, making her hut habi-
table and doing basic chores
took all her time. But she
25　was going to stay.

The children gradually
came out of hiding. Leela

baked sweets and delicacies,
but only one or two suc-
cumbed to the temptation.
30　The Black Witch, the villagers called her — her skin
was darker than theirs. " If
the Black Witch catches
you," the mothers warned,
35　" she will turn you into a
wolf." But daring children
suffered no harm.

Leela addressed the village
council again. The Govern-
40　ment had given her a small
food allowance for the
children, but only for those
who came to her class. All
boys and girls between the
45　ages of three and five were
welcome. Sometimes she
treated them to a handful of
rice and lentils, or a little
porridge, s o m e t i m e s to
50　peanuts or walnuts.

First just a few came.
Then a dozen, then more.
Every morning Leela washed
them at the well — some-
55　thing their mothers did perhaps once or twice a month.
She combed their hair daily,
not just for festivals. If a
child's sleeve was torn, she
60　sewed it on, rather than
leave it to tear further. But
what the mothers appreciated
most was the time they
gained to work in the fields
65　without the children round
their feet.

The day Leela was too ill
to take the class, the village
was thrown into confusion.
70　Parents had come to expect
their new freedom. The
women looked in on her, and
brought her milk and herbal
remedies. Next day she was
75　better.

158

Now Leela felt confident enough to say to one of the mothers: "Your boy is the
80 dirtiest in the class. You should wash him more often."

When he arrived unwashed next day, she sent him home.
85 He missed his porridge. The following morning his face was scrubbed and his wet hair smooth. Leela rewarded him with a smile, and a
90 sliver of soap. She told a girl with a torn frock to come back when it was mended. The mother promptly complied.
95 Leela no longer had to wash the children and mend their clothes — not often, anyway. Their parents had come to depend on her to
100 look after the children, and were prepared to pay her price.

Now Leela could carry out the second stage of her plan.
105 She invited the women to an evening class, to teach them child care. She explained why cleanliness and diet were important. The villagers
110 grew very few vegetables. "You should grow more," she insisted. They asked her why. She improvised : "They increase your blood supply."
115 And flies were bad, she said.

The men told their women-folk to stay away from the class. If they spent their evenings with Leela, the hus-
120 bands would have to carry water and de-husk rice for supper themselves, instead of lounging in the temple square.. The women obeyed reluctantly. The evening 125 classes petered out, but some of the younger wives kept sneaking back. They were curious about the outside world, and wanted to hear 130 more.

The husbands grew angry. Leela was spoiling their wives. Some were even showing signs of rebellion. Where 135 would it end ? The village elders had been right to distrust her from the start. She must go.

They tried again to make 140 life difficult for her, but she remained undaunted. The man who owned her hut decided he wanted it for his relatives. Another villager, one 145 of the few men to appreciate her work, offered her his spare hut.

The children still came to the morning class, even when 150 the food supply gave out, as it often did. She saw that as her major achievement. New habits were being formed. Now, when they were old 155 enough, they were more likely to go to the proper school outside the village rather than graze the cattle. She was getting somewhere. 160

But the villagers continued to plot against her. One day her superiors received an anonymous letter. Soon she was summoned to town. 165 □

(*The Guardian*)

a) Leela came to the village in order to:
   i)   educate the children.
   ii) educate the parents.
   iii) educate the parents as much as the children.

b) The first stage of Leela's plan was to:
   i)   gain the confidence of the children and their parents.
   ii) keep the children clean and well-fed.
   iii) feed only those children who came to her class.

c) The men didn't like Leela because:
   i)   she took up too much of their wives' time.
   ii) they were lazy and she was not.
   iii) their wives were becoming very dependent on her.

⫸→

d) She realised that she had achieved her objectives when:
   i)   she found friends who supported her against the other villagers.
   ii) the children didn't need to be bribed to come to school.
   iii) the children started going to the proper school outside the village.

e) Leela was probably summoned to town because:
   i)   the villagers' traditional way of life was threatened.
   ii) education was thought to be less important than agriculture.
   iii) her superiors wanted to ask her about the contents of the anonymous letter.

Inferring

1 With another student, discuss what you can infer about the following and write down one sentence for each point.

   − the village council
   − the national government
   − village life
   − the woman's role in village society
   − housing and domestic facilities
   − employment
   − Leela's job in general
   − Leela's task in the village

2 What do you think the letter to Leela's superiors contained?

Dealing with unfamiliar words

1 Choose the best answer.

   a) 'dilapidated' (line 15): (i) comfortable, (ii) falling to pieces, (iii) destroyed
      Clue: Leela was an unwanted visitor but a guest all the same. What kind of hut would they put her in?
   b) 'succumbed to' (lines 29–36): (i) gave in to, (ii) resisted, (iii) led into
      Clue: The passage suggests that *all* the children gradually came out of hiding. Does it also suggest that they all accepted her sweets willingly?
   c) 'treated' (line 48): (i) gave essential food, (ii) gave specially prepared food, (iii) gave a special present
      Clue: Do you think it was part of her job to give them these things to eat?
   d) 'complied' (lines 93–4): (i) refused to mend the dress, (ii) argued, (iii) acted as Leela wished
      Clue: At this point in the passage, the mothers were happy for the children to be in class with Leela. So what did this mother have to do for her daughter to be allowed back in school?
   e) 'petered out' (line 126): (i) continued as before, (ii) stopped completely, (iii) occurred less and less frequently until they stopped
      Clue: The men didn't want their wives to go to the class, so the women

160

stopped going. But some of them were still curious about the outside world. So what did they do?

f) 'undaunted' (line 142): (i) unhappy, (ii) undetermined, (iii) unmoved
   Clue: Life was getting very difficult for her in the village. Did she leave immediately?

2 Each word on the left is related in meaning to the group of three words on the right. Choose the word on the right which is most similar in meaning to the one on the left, in the context of this passage.

a) 'suspicious' (line 13)   distrustful   jealous   questionable
b) 'appreciated' (line 63)   grew   respected   were grateful for
c) 'lounging' (line 123)   relaxing   lazing   lying
d) 'curious' (line 129)   interested   odd   inquisitive

3 a) In lines 1–38 find words which mean the same as: behave   children   tasks   brave
  b) In lines 83–102 find words which mean the same as: small piece   rely on
  c) In lines 145–65 find words which mean the same as: accomplishment   called

---

Writing summaries

Imagine that you are Leela's superior. Write a short paragraph describing what she has to do in the village. Give details about local conditions, social customs and life in the village and include details about her tasks. Use no more than 120 words.

Further work

1 Working in pairs, act out the conversation between Leela and her superior when she returned from the village.

2 Work in groups of three or four. Imagine that you are sending some form of aid to the village. Make a list of the things which you think would be most useful.
   Now choose one group in your class to be the national government. Each of the other groups must present its list of things to be sent. Be prepared to justify your choice.

3 Imagine you live in an isolated village. Using ten or twelve words and expressions from the passage, write a short story beginning:

'No one had visited our village for ten years. Then one day a stranger walked into the main square. . .'

Unit 36 Boys are teachers' pets

Predicting

1 Look at the title of the unit. Discuss with another student what you think it means.

2 Now write down 10–15 words which you expect to see in the passage. Can you predict what the passage is likely to say?

3 As you read the passage, answer the questions. Try not to look at the rest of the passage. Check your answers with another student.

    a) Read the first paragraph. Was your prediction correct?

> THE CLASSROOM is a man's world, where boys get two-thirds of the teachers' attention—even when they are in a minority—taunt the girls without punish-
> 5 ment, and receive praise for sloppy work that would not be tolerated from girls. They are accustomed to being teachers' pets, and, if girls get anything like equal treatment, they will protest vehemently and even wreck lessons. 10

    b) So if boys are better treated in class, which would be better: single-sex classes or co-educational classes?

> These claims are made in a book out this week, written by Dale Spender, a lecturer at the London University Institute of Education. She argues that dis- crimination against girls is so deeply 15 embedded in co-educational schools that single-sex classes are the only answer.

    c) How do you think the researcher obtained the evidence for these claims?

> Her case is based on tape-recordings of her own and other teachers' lessons.
> 20 Many of them, like Spender, had delib- erately set out to give girls a fair chance. "Sometimes," says Spender, "I have even thought I have gone too far and have spent *more* time with the girls than
> 25 the boys." The tapes proved otherwise. In 10 taped lessons (in secondary school and college), Spender never gave the girls more than 42 per cent of her attention (the average was 38 per cent) and never 30 gave the boys less than 58 per cent. There were similar results for other teachers, both male and female.

    d) What do you expect the passage to say about the boys' reactions when girls are given more attention?

In other words, when teachers give
35 girls more than a third of their time, they
feel that they are cheating the boys of
their rightful share. And so do the boys
themselves. "She always asks the girls all
the questions," said one boy in a class-
40 room where 34 per cent of the teachers'
time was allocated to girls. "She doesn't
like boys, and just listens to the girls,"
said a boy in another class, where his sex
got 63 per cent of teacher attention.

Boys regarded two-thirds of the 45
teacher's time as a fair deal—and when
they got less they caused trouble in class
and even complained to higher authority.
"It's important to keep their attention,"
said one teacher. "Otherwise, they play 50
you up something awful."

e) What do you expect the passage to say about boys who protest or
challenge the teacher? What will it say about girls who do the same?

According to Spender's research,
double standards pervade the classroom.
"When boys ask questions, protest, or
55 challenge the teacher, they are often met
with respect and rewards; when girls
engage in exactly the same behaviour,
they are often met with punishment and
rebuke."
60 A boy seeking attention will quickly
get a response from a teacher. "But girls
can be fobbed off; their hands can be
held up for ages, and their often polite
requests for assistance can go unheeded
as the teacher is obliged to remain with 65
the boys."

One girl, talking about a male teacher,
commented: "You wouldn't want to
have your hand up to tell him there was a
fire, if you were a girl. We'd all burn to 70
death before he asked you what you
wanted to say."

f) If a teacher is given written work and told it was done by a boy rather
than a girl, do you think it will get more marks?

Boys' written work, too, is judged by
different standards, says Spender. When
75 she asked teachers to mark essays and
projects, the *same* work got better marks
when teachers were told that it came
from boys. "When a boy decides to make
a thing of it, there's not a girl that can
80 stand up to him," one teacher said of a
project on inventions. But, in fact, the
work had been done by a girl.

Neat and tidy work from girls was
treated with some contempt. "I think she
could have spent more time on getting 85
some facts than on making it look
pretty," was one comment. "Typical,
isn't it? All that effort just to make it
look nice—you can't beat girls for being
concerned with appearances," was an- 90
other. But when Spender indicated that
the same work came from a boy, the tune
changed dramatically.

g) In mixed classes, how are teachers likely to react to girls if they are
(i) boisterous, (ii) quiet?

Spender concludes that, in mixed
95 classes, the dice are loaded against the
girls. If they are as boisterous and pushy
as the boys, they are considered "unlady-
like"; if they are docile and quiet, they
are ignored.

h) What is the researcher's conclusion likely to be?

100 A few schools have introduced single-
sex groups for maths and science, says
Spender, and have found significant
improvements in girls' results. Sexual
segregation within schools for certain
subjects—rather than a return to single- 105
sex schools—is the most hopeful solution
she suggests.

(Peter Wilby in *The Sunday Times*)

4 Check whether the words you predicted in 2 appeared in the text. If they didn't,
discuss with your partner whether they might have.

Dealing with unfamiliar words

1 Choose the best answer.

   a) 'taunt the girls' (line 4): This is likely to mean (i) be pleasant, (ii) be unpleasant to the girls.
   b) 'sloppy work' (line 5): This is likely to mean (i) careful, (ii) careless work.
   c) 'vehemently' (line 9): To protest vehemently probably means (i) to complain strongly, (ii) to sulk.
   d) 'deeply embedded' (lines 15–16): This is probably (i) an integral part, (ii) a separate element of co-educational schools.
   e) 'allocated to' (line 41): This means (i) taken from, (ii) given to, (iii) shared with.
   f) 'rebuke' (line 59): When you rebuke someone, you are likely to (i) tell them off, (ii) praise them.
   g) 'unheeded' (line 64): Here, the polite requests for assistance are (i) answered, (ii) ignored.
   h) 'boisterous and pushy' (line 96): This means (i) noisy and ambitious, (ii) dull and uninteresting, (iii) intelligent and inquisitive, (iv) stupid and silent.

2 The following expressions are idiomatic or colloquial English, but their general sense can be understood from the context. Write down what you think they mean.

   a) '. . .they play you up something. . .' (lines 50–1)
   b) 'But girls can be fobbed off. . .' (lines 61–2)
   c) '. . .you can't beat girls for being concerned with appearances. . .' (lines 89–90)
   d) '. . .the tune changed dramatically.' (lines 92–3)
   e) '. . .the dice are loaded against girls.' (lines 95–6)

Check your answers with another student. Do you both agree? You can use your dictionary or ask your teacher whether you guessed correctly.

Writing summaries

1 Choose the best summary of the *argument* of the passage.

   a) Research has shown that boys demand and receive more attention and are better rewarded than girls.
   b) A researcher has recorded ten of her own lessons and has realised that even she cannot avoid giving boys better treatment than girls.
   c) It is claimed that girls obtain only a third of the teacher's time in class and are more easily ignored than boys.
   d) Research suggests that boys and girls are treated differently by their teachers; boys are more active and girls more passive, and the teachers reinforce these learning characteristics.

2 Now choose the best summary of its *conclusion*.

   a) Girls should be segregated from boys for certain subjects, for example maths and science.
   b) Unfortunately there is little chance of returning to single-sex schools and as a result, girls' education will suffer.
   c) If girls' results are to improve, they must be segregated from the boys.
   d) The chances of girls ever doing as well as boys in co-educational classes are not very favourable.

3 Read the passage again and make notes on the following points.

   – the basis of the research
   – teachers' attention to boys and girls
   – teachers' attitude towards their pupils in class
   – teachers' attitude towards their pupils' written work

   The article tends to make the same points in several different ways, because it is reporting on research findings. Read your notes again and cross out any repetitions.

4 Now using the *argument* and the *conclusion* you chose in 1 and 2, and the notes you made in 3, write a summary of the article in 120 words.
   When you have finished, read the article again and check that you have included all the relevant information.

Further work

1 Work in groups of two or three.
   If you are no longer at secondary school find out how many people in your class were taught in single-sex and how many in co-educational classes. Do you or your colleagues agree with the researcher's conclusions? Do you *now* prefer to be taught in single-sex or co-educational classes? Discuss your conclusions with the rest of the class.

   If you are still at secondary school, do you prefer to be taught in single-sex or co-educational classes? Do you think it makes any difference? Have you ever experienced favouritism by the teacher towards boys or girls? Do you agree with the researcher's conclusion? Discuss your conclusions with the rest of the class.

2 Look back over the passage in this unit and, if you have read them, the passages in units 34 and 35. Note down twenty or so words and expressions you have learnt. Then, using as much of the new vocabulary as possible, write a paragraph or two on one of the following subjects:

   – The ideal school.
   – How should school prepare you for a working life?
   – Education outside the school room. Is it useful?

Unit 37   Good taste, bad taste

Predicting

1 The passage in this unit is about taste in design. Before you read it, look at the words below.

inappropriate	simple
refined	excessive
vulgar	pretentious
restrained	confused
neat	dignified

Which words would you use to describe the things you consider to be in good taste? Which ones for things in bad taste? Discuss your answers with another student.

2 Now look at the pictures below. Which would you expect to be described as in *good* or in *bad* taste?

Inferring

Read the passage and then put a tick in the suitable box of the chart on page 170 according to whether the writer thinks the items are in good taste or show no taste.

THE THINGS YOU own tell stories about you as surely as the Joneses you're keeping up with. Each purchase reveals
5 something your partner or closest friend may not realise from your intimate exchanges. Every time you buy something you exercise your *taste*.
10   Before the age of mass production, taste used to be the province of an educated elite. But when the entire population became consumers for the first
15 time, taste came out of the salons and onto the streets. Suddenly, everybody had the opportunity to make a choice.

There cannot objectively be
20 such a thing as "good" or "bad". It is rather as the novelist Arnold Bennett put it: good taste might be better than bad, but bad taste is certainly better than no
25 taste at all.

Exercising taste is not difficult. You decide what stories you want your possessions to tell and then get on and orches-
30 trate them. But be warned: not every story is a flattering one. Buy an onyx ashtray and you might as well rent poster space and tell the world "I am the
35 dupe of cynical manipulators who have succeeded in seducing me with flashy rubbish".

Since the 18th century when taste was first discussed, people
40 have believed that it was an endowment of an elite, handed down to those poor souls below who wanted to better them-

selves. This opened up the market to tastemakers – either 45 the patrician bureaucrats of Victoria's reign, or the teams of slick decorators of today who have made careers out of introducing new money to old 50 furniture.

But is the question of taste just one of household hints? No. Taste is an expression of a whole system of values. And 55 that means yours.

To achieve an understanding of taste means that you should have conviction in your choices. If you look at the 60 history of taste you will see that it is like a sketch of the history of civilisation: for 200 years rococo, classical, gothic, streamlined and then Laura 65 Ashley have all in turn been acceptable expressions of taste. Only gifted artists and designers can predict these changes but anyone can under- 70 stand the principles. Although the history of taste has been one of change, confrontation and reversal, certain patterns constantly recur. Learn these 75 and you're in there with the tastemakers.

The rules are simple. No taste is to acquiesce and act like a pygmy enchanted by 80 beads and mirrors. With no taste you take what is offered and leave your soul undisturbed. Good taste is to care and to choose, to make your 85 own surroundings and even your own appearance more pleasing and more interesting by positive acts of discrimination.

Underpinning what is always thought to be good taste are recurrent ideas such as refinement, restraint, appropriateness and good manners. These all lead to delight; the alternative is vulgar excess which is ultimately unsatisfying.

So, bear these ideas in mind and look at what you own and think about the stories your possessions are telling.

• Why do you have a *gold* wristwatch? This metal is inappropriate for the intended purpose. Steel or plastic is better. Perhaps you want to look like a prosperous arms dealer . . .

• Your Constable reproduction in a pseudo-something frame says "I know nothing about art and care less". A Heineken poster would have been more discriminating.

• Your carpet with its hideous pattern was designed to do one thing only: disguise dirt. Would you not be prouder with a clean simple colour?

• Your choice of the "Honesty" pattern toaster declares you to be the sort of person who will cheerfully admit: "I love buying cynical junk. Anything the marketing department does is good enough for me . . ." If "country kitchen" is the style you want, you'd be better off buying a griddle.

These products are all dishonest. They would rarely be chosen by people with genuine bad taste and never by people with good. They would be purchased only by people with no taste at all . . . and no taste at all means the same as "I don't care".

In the future you will be exposed to more and more choice, not less. As the speed of change brings design nearer to fashion, then decisions about taste will have to be made more and more regularly.

At first this will lead to an even greater profusion of choice, perhaps even more than during the explosion of production and consumption during the consumer revolution of 100 and more years ago. But soon people will find that when anything goes . . . not much really does.

When more consumers exercise taste, manufacturers will be required to make better and more dignified products. It cannot be long before it is generally realised that perfect proportions and understated elegance are superior to meretricious ornament, flashy surfaces and products outstanding only for the degree of social pretentiousness they exude.

If you think about it you will find that you *prefer* neatness and restraint. In the end these qualities are more rewarding than confusion and excess. And, remember, taste is by no means a matter of expense: a slice of good Cheddar is better than many an expensive meal.

These are the Rules of Taste: refinement, restraint, appropriateness and good manners.

Dare you be without them? •

(Stephen Bayley in the *Sunday Express Magazine*)

	good taste	*no taste*
onyx ashtray		
Rococo		
classical		
Gothic		
streamlined		
Laura Ashley		
gold wristwatch		
Constable reproduction		
Heineken poster		
'Honesty' pattern toaster		
Cheddar cheese		

Dealing with unfamiliar words

1 There may be a number of words which you don't understand. In this particular passage, it may only be necessary to guess whether they describe positive or negative qualities. Look at the following words and put a + sign by them if they are positive, and a − sign if they are negative in the context of the passage.

a) 'dupe' (line 35)
b) 'cynical manipulators' (line 35)
c) 'flashy' (line 37)
d) 'slick' (line 48)
e) 'gifted' (line 68)

f) 'cynical junk' (line 125)
g) 'dignified' (line 160)
h) 'understated elegance' (lines 163–4)
i) 'meretricious ornament' (line 165)
j) 'social pretentiousness' (line 168)

2 Now answer the following questions.

a) 'orchestrate' (line 29): This is usually used when a composer adapts a piece of music for the orchestra. It probably means (i) organise, (ii) choose.
b) 'endowment' (line 41): This usually means a gift of money to an institution or a person. Here it means (i) a quality you are born with, (ii) a skill you are taught.
c) 'acquiesce' (line 79): This is likely to mean (i) to react against something, (ii) to accept something calmly.
d) 'underpinning' (line 91): Good taste is underpinned by refinement etc. It means (i) supporting, (ii) opposing.
e) 'griddle' (line 130): This is likely to be a piece of kitchen equipment which is (i) old-fashioned, (ii) modern.

170

f) 'greater profusion' (line 148): This means that there will be even (i) more choice, (ii) less choice.
g) understated (lines 163–4): In the context the elegance is (i) subtle, (ii) exaggerated.
h) meretricious (line 165): In the context, this is another word for (i) elegant, (ii) vulgar.
i) pretentiousness (line 168): The writer sees this as something negative. Social pretentiousness is likely to be (i) elegant manners, (ii) artificial behaviour.

Understanding writer's style

One of the features of the writer's style in this passage is his use of *metaphors* and *similes*.

A *metaphor* is when you use words to indicate something different from the literal meaning.
For example: '. . .taste came out of the salons and onto the streets.' (lines 15–16)
This means that taste was no longer the private property of the rich and sophisticated, but available to the general public as well.

A *simile* is when you liken one thing to another.
For example: '. . .act like a pygmy enchanted by beads and mirrors.' (lines 80–1)
This means to behave in an unsophisticated manner.

Look at the following extracts and decide what they mean.

a) '. . .as the Joneses you're keeping up with.' (lines 2–4)
b) '. . .you might as well rent poster space. . .' (lines 32–3)
c) '. . .I am the dupe of cynical manipulators who have succeeded in seducing me with flashy rubbish.' (lines 34–7)
d) '. . .who have made careers out of introducing new money to old furniture.' (lines 48–51)
e) '. . .and think about the stories your possessions are telling.' (lines 100–2)

Further work

Think of a person, a building and a personal possession. Using ten to fifteen words or expressions from the passage, write a paragraph describing why you think they have or are in good/bad taste.

Unit 38   Shot at dawn

Understanding text organisation

Only the first and last paragraphs of this passage are in the correct position. Read the passage and put the other paragraphs in the right order.

A   THE DAY was particularly grey as we sat waiting to board the plane, and in that depressing light our task seemed more than ever unlikely. We were to
5 shoot dreamy fashion photographs in a dream hotel, set in a distant and exotic land. I gathered together the magic ingredients, an assortment of precious silks and satins, a casket of glittering
10 jewels and pots of shimmering colour. But as I sat in the airport perched on the suitcase which contained all these treasures and gazed at the jeans-clad Cinderella who was destined to be the
15 princess of this piece, I wondered if the glass slippers would fit. Lyn, the model, lay sprawled across a chair, her long legs clad in ragged denim, one snea-kered foot tapping in time to the music
20 which poured from the earphones planted firmly on her head – and which were to remain there all the way to Egypt.

B   On a photographic session the day
25 starts early to catch the best light. By the time dawn broke, work had already started as Jo began to apply a full evening make-up and Simon curled and brushed and combed Lyn's hair
30 into place. Lyn shrugged on a cloak of sophistication as easily as her dress. As we left the room, a lone Egyptian stood in the corridor propped against a cart laden with brushes, brooms and clean
35 linen. His mouth dropped lower and

lower as five of us trooped out of the small room, and when Lyn finally ap-peared, resplendent in a dress encrusted with sequins, her mouth painted a bril-
40 liant crimson and her eyes shadowed with dusky violet, his composure de-serted him. He followed us all the way to the lift staring fixedly at her feet. From beneath the hem of her expensive
45 evening gown there peeked a pair of very dirty white sneakers. In her hands she clutched a pair of black high heels. The lift doors closed on his astonished face. When we returned to change for
50 the next shot there were four more cleaning carts in a circle around our room, and six curious faces. There they remained, day in and day out. That room must have been the cleanest in
55 Egypt.

C   Help arrived at last and we were swept off to our hotel, which did in-deed turn out to be the glorious lo-cation we had been promised. It was
60 built originally as a palace to house the Empress Eugenie and her guests at the inauguration of the Suez Canal. In the dim light it seemed to float tranquilly on the banks of the Nile, among gar-
65 dens of swaying palms and ferns.

D   On the last day, we were shooting the photograph for the cover. Lyn was kneeling in a fountain wearing a silk swimsuit dotted with palm trees, as

172

70 well as long evening gloves and a mass
of diamanté jewellery. I was under the
spray of the fountain trying to protect
her hair from the water, Simon was
perched precariously on the top regul-
75 ating the flow, while Jo was balanced
on the marble rim carefully bouncing
light with a reflector board. This was
to be the most dramatic shot. Everything was perfect, the light was just
80 right and Eva had her camera poised.

E   Our behaviour over the week was so
peculiar that by the third day the
crowd of curious onlookers had become unmanageably large. The hotel
85 security staff were called in. Ten uni-
formed gentlemen appeared – and
promptly joined the rest of the crowd
staring at these mad English cavorting
in the midday sun.

F   We arrived at midnight amidst the
heat, the babble and the strange, sweet
smells of Cairo. The promised car was
not there to meet us, so we loitered
furtively among the crowds. They cir-
95 cled and swooped around us curiously,
for we were a strange sight. There was
Lyn, merrily jiggling to her private

music; Eva, the photographer, laden
with expensive equipment; Simon, the
100 hairdresser, whose undoubted beauty
and curling blond hair as long as a
girl's aroused comments in his own
country, let alone the Middle East. Jo,
the make-up artist, is a pretty and in-
105 fectiously happy girl who insisted on
smiling beckoningly at every sinister
stranger while I, fashion editor and
mother-elect of the team, whirled pro-
tectively round them all frantically
110 looking for change for the telephone.

G   Suddenly the head security guard
made frantic motioning signals at me.
We all stopped. He led me wordlessly
to the enormous swimming pool and
115 with an enormous sweeping gesture
showed me its glittering blue depths.
Then he explained in fragmented
English that while he could see we
were enjoying our holiday, if we wanted
120 to swim this was probably a better
place. I looked down at my dripping
wet clothes then gazed over at the
team, all balanced in ludicrous positions
around that exquisite marble fountain,
125 and smiled sweetly at him. Some
dreams are surreal.

(Sally Brampton in *The Observer Colour Magazine*)

Checking comprehension

Answer the following questions on the passage.

a) What was the aim of the trip to Cairo?
b) How many people went on the trip?
c) Why did the writer go on the trip?
d) What happened when they first arrived at the airport?
e) What was the location for the fashion photographs?
f) Why did they have to start work so early?
g) What was the effect of the fashion team on the hotel staff?
h) Why did the fashion team attract so much attention?
i) Why did the model appear particularly strange?
j) Who called in the hotel staff?
k) How many photographs had they taken round the fountain before they were
interrupted on the last day?

Dealing with unfamiliar words

1 Write down all the nouns used to refer to clothes and shoes.

2 Write down all the words and expressions used to describe people's physical appearance.

Understanding writer's style

1 The writer sometimes uses expressions made up of words which mean more or less the same thing.
   For example: '. . .staring fixedly at. . .' (line 43). The word 'stare' means to look at something without moving one's eyes, and the adverb 'fixedly' only repeats the idea conveyed by 'stare'. Some readers may find this kind of repetition rather distracting; others may find it an effective way of reinforcing what is being described.

   Look at the phrases below and decide whether you find that the words in italics add something to what is being described. Use a dictionary if there are any words which you don't understand.

   a) '*glittering* jewels' (lines 9–10)
   b) '*shimmering* colour' (line 10)
   c) 'planted *firmly*' (line 21)
   d) 'dress *encrusted* with sequins' (lines 38–9)
   e) 'float *tranquilly*' (line 63)
   f) 'perched *precariously*' (line 74)
   g) '*infectiously* happy' (lines 104–5)
   h) 'frantic *motioning* signals' (line 112)
   i) 'enormous *sweeping* gesture' (line 115)
   j) '*dripping* wet clothes' (lines 121–2)

   Remember that there is no right or wrong answer to this exercise; it is simply a matter of discussing what you personally find effective.

2 What does the writer mean by the following phrases?
   a) '. . .the jeans-clad Cinderella who was destined to be the princess of this piece. . .' (lines 13–15)
   b) '. . .Lyn shrugged on a cloak of sophistication as easily as her dress.' (lines 30–1)
   c) '. . .I, fashion editor and mother-elect of the team. . .' (lines 107–8)
   d) 'Some dreams are surreal.' (lines 125–6)

3 The writer also uses more literary or poetic words than you might find in
   everyday speech. Find everyday equivalents for these words.

   a) 'treasures' (line 13)   e) 'tranquilly' (line 63)
   b) 'dusky' (line 41)   f) 'poised' (line 80)
   c) 'peeked' (line 45)   g) 'babble' (line 91)
   d) 'clutched' (line 47)

Evaluating the text

The stylistic features which you looked at in *Understanding writer's style* all
combine to emphasise the contrast between the *dream*: luxury, elegance etc. and
the *reality*: the crowds, hotel cleaners, officials etc. Even the onlookers, it seems,
recognised the dream quality of the photographic session.

Re-read the passage and pick out two or three more sentences which refer to the
dream, and two or three which refer to the *reality*.

Further work

Choose ten to fifteen words or expressions from the passage and then use them in a
paragraph describing a dream-like occasion. Try and describe the occasion in as
much detail as possible, and also how you felt when you returned to reality.

Unit 39   Absolute musts

Understanding text organisation

1   Work in pairs. Look at the pictures below. Try and decide what the items are.

1

2

3

4

2 Match the following titles of the items with their pictures and their descriptions.

- Pet-a-vision
- Cap for two
- Dance instruction shoes
- Woofer
- Garbage shoot
- Solarmuffs

3 The sentences below are taken from the descriptions of the six items shown in the illustrations. Separate the six descriptions and match them with the items.

a) A personal solar-powered warming system that will keep your ears toasty regardless of outside temperature, the natural way.

b) Double your pleasure, comfort, convenience and economy with this broadminded, all-wool visor cap.

c) A foolproof method for learning even the most complex steps.

d) Enables you and your 'capmate' to converse quietly despite the high ambient sound levels, stay together in a crowd, and respond simultaneously to the same sensory stimulation.

e) Direct disposal system saves thousands of dollars over existing garbage collection services.

f) Also excellent for 'trying out' a potential relationship before a more complex commitment is undertaken.

g) A long overdue audio appliance is this 'hands off' portable stereo radio.   ⟫⟩→

h)   This non-organic home companion brings all the joy of pet ownership
      with none of the mess.

i)   Solar collector unit may be angled to most effectively trap sun's rays and
      unit is compatible with most headgear.

j)   You dance as well as your partner immediately, regardless of previous
      experience or sense of rhythm.

k)   Folds compactly for pocket-carrying.

l)   Let Rover earn his keep while his master dances, skates or just keeps time
      to his favourite music with unimpaired articulation of the limbs.

m) The antics of your 'fuzzy friend' will amuse you for hours.

n)   Biodegradable projectile is loaded with garbage and placed into
      launching tube, hatch is securely closed, plunger pulled back and
      released – and garbage is shot to disposal area.

o)   If it's your first time on the floor for both partners, you learn together, at
      the same pace, so interest is maintained.

p)   It's fast, sanitary and economical.

q)   Pet is soothed by music for 'better luck' on the walk.

r)   Realistic programming even includes restlessness at feeding time.

s)   Unit is pre-aimed by city inspectors to prevent misuse.

t)   Electronic format allows access to entire animal kingdom, a boon to those
      with a flair for the exotic.

u)   Taps available for advanced students.

   (*Philip Garner's Better Living Catalog*)

4 Which items do the following footnotes refer to?

   Note: use conventional muffs for overcast conditions at night.

   To determine size, add hat sizes of both parties, then subtract .074.

   Projectile available in budget-priced ten-pack.

Reacting to the text

1 The descriptions of the products emphasise their advantages. Can you think of
   any others which aren't mentioned?

2 However, they neglect to mention any disadvantages. Can you think of any?

Understanding writer's style

1 A feature of the style in these advertisements is the use of long or scientific-sounding phrases instead of more common words. This kind of jargon is often used in advertising to make something ordinary sound more significant.

Discuss with your partner how you could say the following expressions in a simpler way.

a) 'Enables you and your "capmate" to converse quietly despite the high ambient sound levels. . .' (sentence d)
b) 'A long overdue audio appliance. . .' (sentence g)
c) '. . .This non-organic home companion. . .' (sentence h)
d) '. . .unit is compatible with most headgear.' (sentence i)
e) 'Folds compactly for pocket-carrying.' (sentence k)
f) '. . .with unimpaired articulation of the limbs.' (sentence l)

2 Clearly neither the items nor the descriptions are meant to be taken seriously. For example: 'Unit is pre-aimed by city inspectors to prevent misuse'. (sentence s) Can you imagine what might happen if the unit wasn't pre-aimed? What do the advertisements suggest by the following phrases?

a) 'Also excellent for "trying out" a potential relationship before a more complex commitment is undertaken.' (sentence f)
b) '. . .with none of the mess.' (sentence h)
c) 'Let Rover earn his keep. . .' (sentence l)
d) 'Realistic programming even includes restlessness at feeding time.' (sentence r)
e) 'Electronic format allows access to the entire animal kingdom. . .' (sentence t)
f) 'Taps available for advanced students.' (sentence u)

Checking comprehension

The 'products' come from a book called *The Better Living Catalog*. The passage on the next page gives a brief explanation of why the book was written. Read it and then answer the questions below. Use your own words.

a) According to the passage, what are the illustrations and text in *The Better Living Catalog* meant to resemble?
b) Where do you usually find this kind of advertisement?
c) How would you describe the style of the advertisements?
d) How is the demand for this merchandise created?
e) In what way are the advertisements in *The Better Living Catalog* different from the usual advertisements of this kind of merchandise?
f) What is the effect of the products in *The Better Living Catalog* on the consumer?

Somewhere in the hinterlands of all newspapers of any pride and substance there is a section that in sheer flair and inventiveness often out-
5 shines the front page. Under some such rubric as Mini-Mart, there burgeons a riotous undergrowth of small display advertisements, lavishly illustrated with line draw-
10 ings, that contain a greater range of exotic merchandise than Aladdin's cave.

These advertisements represent an entire sub-culture, complete
15 down to its own language and symbols. Its descriptive content is exclusively in the superlative, its only grammar the exclamation mark. The common denominator of all on
20 offer is that it is irresistibly life-enhancing in a truly singular way. The merchandise constantly fulfils the demand created because it is a demand that almost invariably did
25 not exist before the advertisement appeared.

In such a limitlessly promising consumer field, of course, the Americans are pre-eminent and it
30 comes as no surprise that an American has produced what may be the definitive example of the genre. The *Better Living Catalog* by Philip Garner, a Los Angeles artist
35 and inventor, consists of 62 "absolute necessities for contemporary survival", all lovingly constructed by their creator so that ACTUAL PHOTOGRAPHS! of them are
40 possible, in itself a MAJOR TECHNOLOGICAL ADVANCE! over the old wood block and line-drawing.

Garner, a serious artist with more formal work on show in lead-
45 ing American galleries and museums, has extended the same careful detailing to a text in small-ad-speak of pinpoint accuracy.

"Double your pleasure, comfort, convenience and economy
50 with this broad-minded, all-wool visor cap," he appends to the Cap for TWO! "Enables you and your 'cap-mate' to converse quietly despite high ambient sound levels,
55 *stay together* in a crowd and respond simultaneously to the same sensory stimulation. Also excellent for 'trying out' a potential relationship before a more complex commitment
60 is undertaken." Even the convention of a complicated, small-print post-script is not forgotten: "To determine size, add hat sizes of both parties, then subtract ·074."
65 The cumulative effect of 62 such assaults on the popular conception of consumer sanity ("Only a small selection shown here. Many more in stock!") is a familiar one to all
70 devotees of the Postal Bargain: an astonished regard for such a brilliant notion, followed by a powerful desire to send off for one.

If the *Better Living Catalog* (to
75 be published here in September by Sidgwick & Jackson, £3·95) is under-pinned by a serious intent to reflect the excesses of rampant materialism, the message has to
80 compete with that irresistible urge. ∎

(John Sandilands in *The Sunday Times Colour Magazine*)

Further work

1 Work in groups of two or three. Look at the following illustrations from *The Better Living Catalog*. Decide what they could be used for and write a short advertisement for each one. Include a title and a description of its features.

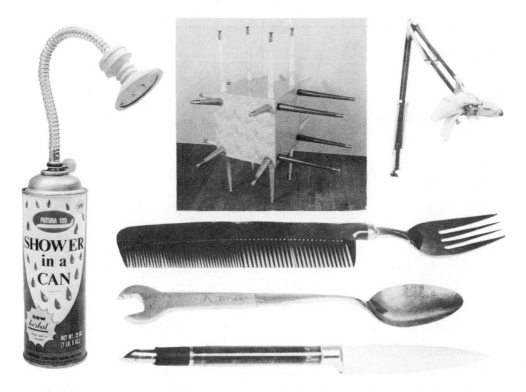

2 Think of an invention of your own which will make life easier. Choose ten to fifteen words and expressions from this unit and use them in a description of your invention.

3 Look through the passages in this unit again and, if you have read them, the passages in units 37 and 38. Note down twenty or so words and expressions which you have learnt. Using as much of this new vocabulary as possible write a paragraph or two on one of the following subjects:
   – 'It doesn't matter what something looks like just as long as it does what it's meant to do.'
   – Describe your favourite fashion in clothes.

Unit 40 Trials and errors

Predicting

1 The following passage discusses some of the differences in the legal systems of Britain, France and the United States of America. Before you read it, decide which of the following words you would expect to find in the passage. If you do not understand all the words, check their meaning in a dictionary.

tyrant	platform	plaintiff
defence	lawyer	cabinet
president	polytechnic	bench
statement	witness	prologue
libel	evidence	chancellor
prosecution	criminal	trial
tournament	fine	

2 Now check with another student to see whether you have chosen the same words.

3 Read the passage and check whether the words you chose in 1 appeared or not.

HOW EFFICIENT is our own system of criminal trial? Does it really do the basic job we ask of it – convicting the guilty and
5 acquitting the innocent? It is often said that the British trial system is more like a game than a serious attempt to do justice. The lawyers on each side are
10 so engrossed in playing hard to win, challenging each other and the judge on technical points, that the object of finding out the truth is almost forgotten.
15 All the effort is concentrated on the big day, on the dramatic cross-examination of the key witnesses in front of the jury.

Critics like to compare our 'adversarial' system (resemb-   20
ling two adversaries engaged in a contest) with the Continental 'inquisitorial' system, under which the judge plays a more important inquiring role.   25

In early times, in the Middle Ages, the systems of trial across Europe were similar. At that time trial 'by ordeal' – essen-
tially a religious event – was the   30
main way of testing guilt or innocence. When this was eventually abandoned the two systems parted company. On the Continent church-trained legal   35
officials took over the functions

of both prosecuting and judging, while in England these were largely left to lay people, the justices of the peace and the jury. The jurymen were often illiterate and this meant that all the evidence had to be put to them orally. This historical accident dominates procedure even today, with all evidence being given in open court by word of mouth on the crucial day.

On the other hand, in France for instance, all the evidence is written down before the trial under supervision by an investigating judge. This exhaustive pre-trial investigation is said to lessen the risk of sending an innocent person for trial. But to English eyes a French trial looks very undramatic; much of it is just a public checking of the written records already gathered.

The Americans adopted the British system lock, stock and barrel and enshrined it in their Constitution. But, while the basic features of our systems are common, there are now significant differences in the way serious cases are handled. First, because the USA has virtually no contempt of court laws to prevent pre-trial publicity in the newspapers and on television, American lawyers are allowed to question jurors about knowledge and beliefs.

In Britain this is virtually never allowed, and a random selection of jurors who are presumed not to be prejudiced is empanelled. Secondly, there is no separate profession of barrister in the United States, and both prosecution and defence lawyers who are to present cases in court prepare them themselves. They go out and visit the scene, track down and interview witnesses, and familiarise themselves personally with the background. In Britain it is the solicitor who prepares the case, and the barrister who appears in court is not even allowed to meet witnesses beforehand. British barristers also alternate doing both prosecution and defence work. Being kept distant from the preparation and regularly appearing for both sides, barristers are said to avoid becoming too personally involved, and can approach cases more dispassionately. American lawyers, however, often know their cases better.

Reformers rightly want to learn from other countries' mistakes and successes. But what is clear is that justice systems, largely because they are the result of long historical growth, are peculiarly difficult to adapt piecemeal. ●

(Walter Merricks in the *Radio Times*)

Extracting main ideas

Decide which of the following sentences expresses the main idea of the passage.

a) The passage describes how the British legal system works and compares it favourably with other systems.
b) The passage questions whether the system of trial by jury can ever be completely efficient.
c) The passage suggests a number of reforms which should be made to the legal systems of various countries.
d) The passage compares the legal systems of a number of countries and discusses their advantages and disadvantages.
e) The passage describes how efficient the French legal system is in comparison to the British and American systems.

Discuss your choice with another student.

Inferring

1 Discuss what evidence there is in the passage for the following statements. If there is no evidence, explain what the passage really says.

a) The British legal system is often considered to be not very fair.
b) Lawyers in Britain are prepared to lie in order to win their case.
c) In the adversarial system, it is the lawyers who play the leading roles.
d) When trial by ordeal was finally abandoned throughout Europe, trial by jury was introduced.
e) Oral evidence was unnecessary in France because the judges and prosecutors could read.
f) It is said that oral evidence tends to increase the risk of bringing the wrong person to trial.
g) In France, the trial itself is merely a formality.
h) In Britain, newspapers are not allowed to publish details about the trial before it takes place.
i) In America, lawyers question jurors in an attempt to ensure that they are not prejudiced.
j) In Britain, barristers do not attempt to familiarise themselves with the case.
k) American lawyers tend to be more passionately involved in their cases.
l) In general, it would be impossible to introduce a total reform of the legal systems of the countries mentioned.

2 What's the difference between a *judge* and a *lawyer*? Use your dictionary if
   necessary.
   What do you think the judge's role in Britain and the USA is?
   What do you think the lawyer's role in France is?

Dealing with unfamiliar words

1 A number of legal concepts may be difficult to understand. Remember that it is
   sometimes quite difficult to find the exact equivalent in the legal terminology of
   your own language. In this passage the writer helps by explaining the following
   concepts elsewhere in the passage. Answer the questions by looking at the
   passage again.

   a) In the 'adversarial' system (line 20), who do you think are the adversaries?
   b) In the 'inquisitorial' system (line 23), who do you think is the inquisitor?
   c) What example is given of 'contempt of court' (line 72)?
   d) What do you think a solicitor does?
   e) What do you think a barrister does?

2 a) In paragraphs 1 and 2, find words which mean the same as:
       involved   unable to read or write.
   b) In paragraphs 3 and 4, find words which mean the same as:
       thorough   included.
   c) In paragraphs 5 and 6, find words or expressions which mean the same as:
       get to know   without taking sides.

3 Look at these idiomatic expressions in the passage. Discuss what you think they
   might mean.

   a) 'parted company' (line 34)   c) 'lock, stock and barrel' (lines 64–5)
   b) 'by word of mouth' (line 48)   d) 'piecemeal' (line 115)

Writing summaries

1 Read the passage again and write notes in the chart on the following features of
   the legal system mentioned. Remember that not all the boxes can be filled in.

	Britain	*USA*	*France*
'adversarial' system			
'inquisitorial' system			
written evidence in court			
oral evidence in court			
contempt of court laws			
random selection of juries			
role of barrister/solicitor/lawyer			

2 Choose the best summary of lines 1–25.
   a) The writer questions whether the British trial system is efficient because the
      lawyers are more concerned with winning the case than finding out the truth.
   b) In the writer's opinion, the British trial system is too much like a game to be
      really efficient.

3 Now choose the best summary of lines 108–15.
   a) The writer concludes that justice systems are difficult to reform.
   b) The writer concludes by saying that justice systems could only be improved if
      they were totally reformed.

4 Using your notes and your answers to the questions above, write a summary of
   the passage in 120–150 words.

Further work

1 *If you are in a class of people from different countries*, discuss whether the systems of justice in your countries are adversarial or inquisitorial. Find out which of the features mentioned in the passage also exist in your countries. Prepare a short report comparing the different systems.
   If you are in a class of people from the same country, discuss whether the system of justice in your country is adversarial or inquisitorial. Find out if the features mentioned also exist in your country's system and those of two other countries of your choice. Prepare a short report which compares the systems.

2 Choose ten to fifteen words or expressions from the passage and use them in a short story which begins:

   'As the policeman pushed me into the prison cell, I said "You're making a dreadful mistake. . ."'

Unit 41   Arresting scenes in Bombay

The following passage is about the fight against crime in Bombay, India.

Reading for specific information

Read the passage and make notes about the following points.

– Bombay: its size and population
– types of crime in Bombay

HOW DOES one begin policing Bombay – this hideous, beautiful, protean, polyglot seaport, cramped like Manhattan on
5 an island, stretched between prodigious wealth and craven poverty? It already contains eight million people and every day more than a thousand new
10 migrants arrive – driven from their villages by despair, lured to the city by hope – to join the crowd.
　　Colaba police station is on the
15 front line where the police and public meet. It covers Bombay's two most expensive hotels, a development of luxury apartment blocks, a selection of the most
20 spectacularly overcrowded tenements (they have been known to collapse under the sheer weight of humanity) and some typically abject shanty slums.
25　　The inspector in charge, a Parsi with a reputation for being a tough officer, deplored his lack of equipment; a single jeep is his entire transport for the district.

We went out in it, looking for his 30 men on the beat: past the yacht club, the Gateway of India, the famous old Taj hotel on the waterfront, the seedier backstreet hotels full of hippies (the word 35 seems archaic now except in Bombay where the flavour of the Sixties lingers). The inspector said that morphine is just too easy to get now, making his job harder 40 than ever. He once had an English girl friend, queen of the junkies, who used to bring him information, but she died. The French give most trouble, though the 45 Arabs are catching up. Bombay is a playground for these *nouveaux* millionaires. The inspector hates the Arabs.

　　His constables patrol in fours, 50 day and night. We found two of them at last, under a tree near the Taj; the other two had gone to lunch.

　　Back at the police station he 55 picked up the file of his latest case, unusual even in his experience. A girl had fallen in love with

a boy who worked in the same
60 office. He seduced her, promising to marry her, but broke his
word. She told her family and
they collected five young men
who came in a car, waylaid the
65 boy, tied him up and drove him
off to the marriage pavilion. Seeing his chance of escape he ran
upstairs to the second floor and
jumped from a window into a
70 tree, but the branch broke, he fell
and died in hospital. The girl was
distraught and put on a widow's
white sari, in spite of the fact that
they were never married and she
75 wasn't pregnant. The inspector
found he could charge the men on
four counts: abduction, rioting
(five people constitute a riot),
wrongful restraint and wrongful
80 confinement. He thought that
was enough; besides, the case
brightened the daily round of
beggars, thieves and ponces.

For two days I sat in the charge
85 room – glad to be a volunteer
there, not hauled in from the
street. Colaba is one of the oldest
police stations, haunted by a sense
of finality: the fatal rack of hand-
90 cuffs hanging on the wall, the
heaps of paper, the ancient radio,
often unmanned and crackling
uselessly to itself. The police HQ
with its operations room and
95 computer seems far away in another city, another age. Across
the yard is the lock-up where
dark figures loom behind the
bars. ('Don't make comparisons,'
100 a local journalist said, 'it's probably no worse than the places
where they live.') Pairs of brown
arms sometimes wave out, reach-
ing into freedom; a white pair
105 too, which made me still more
uneasy.

A man was brought in, carrying a couple of bird cages full of
green parrots, charged with
110 trading in the street without a
licence. A beggar, a shuffling
creature from the fringe of humanity, was put into the beggars'
pound; eventually he would be
115 deported from the city. An Arab
came in, dazed with indignation,
to complain that his passport and
5,000 rupees – nearly £325 – had
been stolen. A landlord, with his
120 wife and two sons, was spinning
an intricate tale about a trouble-
some tenant when there was a
sudden shout and scuffle, and a
frightened young man arrived in
125 the charge room, injected from
the street, with a couple of constables.

At once the sub-inspector, a
mild officer hardly older than the
130 youth, turned ferocious, like a
terrier with a rabbit. Handcuffs
were clapped on and some crisp
punches delivered. The first swift
steps of justice aren't a pleasant
135 sight: blows from the officer and
jabs from a constable with a
bamboo. Questions were barked,
orders snapped, while a clerk
scribbled fiercely in a ledger.
140 Then the youth's trousers were
unhitched; they dropped to the
floor, showing two heavy steel
ball-bearings hanging by string
from his waist, stolen from his
145 employer. Ha! The treasure was
yanked off and put on the table
beside the cage of parrots. More
punches and prods, for emphasis,
before the youth was marched
150 away, manacled to a constable, to
the lock-up.

Later, three women came with
their children and pots of hot
food, and the whiff of curry filled
155 the charge room. It was for husbands, sons, fathers, who had
disappeared into the police station.
The women pleaded but were

»»→

driven away, threatened with being prosecuted for trespass. Prisoners get fed according to the rules, with no extras allowed. In due course, two buckets were fetched with rice and lentils, and dollops of each were handed through the bars.

Towards evening a bearded old man in a turban was brought in, with a small sack and a large basket. A constable took the sack, opened it and lifted out a hedgehog which was soon trotting under the chairs and behind the filing cabinets. The old man was told to put the basket on a desk and take off the lid; a cobra uncoiled and slithered out, round a typewriter and over the telephone, a yard in front of the sub-inspector. It was a test of self-control, a match between officer and snake, and the snake lost. The fine for entertaining the public without a licence is 25 rupees – £1.60. The old man caught his hedgehog and cobra and put them away, then clasped his hands as if in prayer, nearly in tears, and appealed to everyone – sub-inspector, constables, clerk, even myself – for leniency. But he knew he couldn't win.

After two days at Colaba I began to see how it fits into the total scheme. Petty human errors, brought in from the street, are put through the ancient ritual, then reduced to stacks of yellowing paper. But they are specks in the morass of Bombay's crime. The small-time thief, the unlicensed snake-charmer, the drunkard, the pimp, the barefoot American girl with tangled hair and glazed eyes, trailing her private misery among the pavement beggars and shoeshine boys – all are bit-part actors caught up in a colossal show. Even the bent policeman, occasionally tempted beyond endurance, is insignificant; underpaid, probably housed in grim quarters, then called out to a smart hotel or flat, brushing against the gold. It can't be easy for him.

(Nicholas Wollaston in *The Observer Colour Magazine*)

Dealing with unfamiliar words

1 There are likely to be a number of words which you will find difficult to understand in this passage. There isn't room to deal with them all, but here are a few clues to help you guess the general sense of some of them. Try and think of a word or a phrase to explain what the following words mean.

a) 'protean' (line 3): This describes a city which is both hideous and beautiful, very rich and very poor at the same time.

b) 'polyglot' (line 3): This describes a city in which English, French, Arabic and other languages are spoken, as well as Indian languages.

c) 'prodigious' (line 6): In lines 46–7, Bombay is described as being 'a playground for. . .millionaires.' What kind of wealth is prodigious wealth likely to be?

d) 'craven' (line 6), 'abject' (line 24): Do you think these words are meant to lessen or heighten the impression of poverty?

e) 'shanty slums' (line 24): What kind of housing do poor people live in?

f) 'deplored' (line 27): Does the inspector think one jeep is sufficient to his needs?

g) 'junkies' (line 42): What do the words 'hippies' and 'morphine' suggest about the meaning of this word?

h) 'waylaid' (line 64): What did the five young men have to do before tying up the boy and driving him off?

i) 'distraught' (line 72): Why do you think the young woman put on the 'widow's white sari'?

j) 'abduction' (line 77): What was the main action of the young men which led to their arrest?

k) 'unhitched' (line 141): What do you usually have to do to trousers before they can be dropped to the floor?

l) 'yanked off' (line 146): If the steel ball bearings were attached to the youth's waist, what did the policeman have to do before he could put them on the table?

m) 'dollops' (line 165): How do you think the food was presented to the prisoners if it arrived in buckets and was handed through the bars?

n) 'leniency' (line 191): If the old man had been arrested and was now in tears, appealing to everyone, what do you think he was asking for?

o) 'bent' (line 209): If the policeman is occasionally 'tempted beyond endurance', what is likely to happen? Is this acceptable behaviour for a policeman?

2 There may be other words which you don't understand. Use the techniques explained earlier in this book to help you guess their general sense.

Understanding writer's style

There is also a great deal to infer from the writer's choice of words and style. These may have connotations, certain images or references which help the reader to understand the writer's intention better. Working in pairs, answer the following questions.

a) Apart from the fact that Bombay is a polyglot city on an island, why does the writer liken the city to Manhattan? In general, what is the passage about?

b) What does the writer mean by 'driven from their villages by despair, lured to the city by hope'? (lines 10–12)

c) What image is suggested by the expression 'the front line'? (line 15)

d) Why is the police station 'haunted by a sense of finality'? (lines 88–9)

e) '...where dark figures loom behind the bars.' (lines 97–9). What impression does this give of the prison?

f) Why is the beggar in lines 111–13 'a shuffling creature from the fringe of humanity'?

g) What does 'like a terrier with a rabbit' (lines 130–1) suggest about the sub-inspector's behaviour?

h) What does the writer suggest by 'Questions were barked, orders snapped'? (lines 137–8)

i) 'More punches and prods, for emphasis...' (lines 147–8). Does the writer think the violence was necessary?

j) What does the writer mean by describing the crimes in anecdotes as 'petty human errors'? (line 195)

k) Why does he say 'But they are specks in the morass of Bombay's crime'? (lines 199–200)

Evaluating the text

1 Work in pairs. Look back at the crimes you noted down in *Reading for specific information*. Which of these crimes do you regard as serious, and which do you consider to be merely petty offences?

2 Which type of crimes are illustrated by the anecdotes in the passage?

3 Why do you think the writer concentrates on this type of crime?

4 What type of crime would you say that the police force in Bombay is capable of dealing with?

5 How would you describe the attitude of the police force in the face of such crime?

Further work

1 Work in groups of three or four. Discuss what are the most important crimes in your home towns. Choose three of them and note down any suggestions you can make about how to deal with them.
   Now find students with a list of similar crimes. Do they agree with your suggestions for solving the problem? Work together and draw up a common list of proposals.
   Organise a class discussion on ways to beat crime in the cities.

2 Choose ten to fifteen words or expressions from the passage. Use them in an imaginary description of a typical day in the life of a police officer in your town.

Unit 42 Streetwise

In the first passage of this unit, the writer describes what happened to him one evening in London.

Predicting

1 The following words all appear in the passage. Before you read the passage, look at the title and the words. Working in pairs, discuss what you think happened.

across the common
unshaven
my wallet was well-laden
pushed
losing my spectacles
two others who had been sitting on
    the seat

pinned to the ground
held my throat
rolled me over
wallet
cheque card
I watched the three run away
police station

2 Write a few sentences describing what you think happened.

3 Now read the passage.

Twilight robbery on the green

'After the play at the Bush Theatre in West London, I sat outside the pub (the evening of Monday July 2 was hot) for half an hour or so with a friend whom I'd taken to the press night. Doug Lucie's *Progress* was short, and I didn't have to write my review until the end of the week. I hadn't seen Astrid for nearly 20 years, but a fellow critic had taken her to be my wife and there was, absurdly, a degree of embarrassment.

As Astrid and I sat outside the pub, the Shepherd's Bush traffic thundered by. We tried, in a short time, to catch up on our respective lives over the last two decades.

A man with a face like an over-done baked potato lurched above us and asked, most courteously in a sozzled way, if we could spare him a coin. I dipped my hand in my pocket and handed him 10p, which

194

made me feel both philanthropic
and mean.

30 Astrid and I kept talking and the
man continued to swing and lurch
over us, thanking us profusely.

At about 10pm we parted. Astrid
lived near, and turned into
35 Goldhawk Road. With some difficulty (the traffic is relentless), I
crossed Shepherds Bush Green and
began to walk – as I had done
many times before, after a visit to
40 the Bush – across the common
towards the Tube.

The sky was still quite bright,
and I was thinking of Astrid, our
lives in Edinburgh more than 20
45 years before, when I noticed,
without paying much attention, a
man get up from a bench to the left
of the path I trod and who walked,
at a brisk pace, more or less in the
50 direction I was going.

He was stocky, sturdy, scruffy
and unshaven and proved to have
an Irish accent. Suddenly he was in
front of me, close up: "Can you
55 give me a pound?" It half-crossed
my mind that it was no way to beg
a coin. I replied, that I could not.
(For once my wallet was well-
laden; my wife had slipped me the
60 housekeeping before going on
holiday, and I was doling the cash
out to the children on a daily basis:
there lodged about £60 close to my
breast).

65 Whereupon – all this more quickly than I could think – he jostled
me as I tried to push past, assuming
I'd succeed: I was, by an inch or
two, taller than he but he was
70 heavier. His hand shot out and up
and held my Adam's apple, pressed
it and pushed and I was thrust
backwards on to the grass, losing
my spectacles.

75 Somehow the two others who
had been sitting on the seat beside
him were behind me, and I was
pinned to the ground. Swear words
and expletives were spat in my
80 direction with venom. Without my
glasses, I could see little. Had I
thought, perhaps I'd have said:
"Take my wallet, let me be." As it
was, I thrashed about on the ground
85 determined not to lose.

Laughably, my first concern was
for the notes I'd taken at the play:
the pages of my notebook were
strewn about. Then instinct persuaded me to turn on to my 90
stomach, and with right elbow tuc-
ked in I tried to guard my wallet. I
was surprised, as someone who
takes no exercise, how strong I was,
relatively speaking. The first man 95
held my throat, so I couldn't cry
out while the second man held my
arms.

Eventually they rolled me over
and the woman took my wallet. She 100
ran towards the Shepherds Bush
Road with it – taking my Barclaycard, cheque card, and various
membership cards. The men let go
of me (at least I wasn't kicked for 105
luck) and I scrabbled around, trying
to find the notes of my review.
Then I saw my glasses and stood
up, groggily. I watched the three
run away, towards the distant 110
traffic.

I made it to the nearby police
station, and I was driven around the
area to see if I could identify the
brave trio. I could not. The officer 115
took down the particulars, and said
he assumed my assailants were
coloured. I said they seemed to
have Irish accents. "Are you sure
that wasn't a con?" Perhaps, he 120
confided, they were pretending to be
Irish. Maybe they were pretending
to be white, too, I thought.

They'd left, in another pocket,
my Underground pass, and as I 125
travelled home some be-leathered,
sub-Hell's Angels handed out a
leaflet. "Policing London", it began,
"by coercion. The liberties of all
Londoners are again under attack. 130
Protect London: oppose the police
Bill." The man sitting next to me
muttered angrily and asked what I
thought. I hadn't read the new Bill,
I said. 135

At ten to midnight, back home, I
tried to phone Barclaycard. The
number rang and rang. I dialled
again and woke up some
poor man in Northallerton 140
(one digit different), who
said not to worry, it happened eight times a day.

(Giles Gordon in *The Times*)

Extracting main ideas

1 Look back at the passage and decide which of the sentences below best
summarises its main ideas.

   a) The passage describes how well organised muggings in London have become.
   b) The passage questions whether the police give us sufficient protection in our
       everyday lives in the city.
   c) The writer describes the outrage and terror he experienced when he was
       mugged.
   d) The writer relates in a calm way what happened when he was mugged on a
       hot summer's evening.
   e) The writer describes his experience of being mugged and reveals a certain
       sympathy for his attackers.
   f) The passage relates the plight of down-and-outs in London, and deplores the
       fact that more is not done to help them.

2 Look back at what you wrote in *Predicting*, 2. Discuss with your partner
whether you accurately predicted the story.

Inferring

Decide what evidence there is in the passage for the following statements. If there is
no evidence, explain what the passage actually says.

a) The writer is a theatre critic.
b) He was going out with an old girl friend because his wife was away.
c) The writer had mixed feelings about giving money to the first old man.
d) He didn't give anything to the second man.
e) The reaction of the second man took him by surprise.
f) The writer didn't see the other two people until they attacked him.
g) Fortunately the attack was not more violent than was absolutely necessary.
h) The policeman thought most muggings were done by Irishmen or coloured
    people.
i) The police were not particularly helpful.
j) The policeman who took down the details of the assault had a racist attitude.
k) He concludes that he is in favour of the new bill to restrict the powers of the
    police.

The second passage is also about mugging, but the subject is treated in a more
lighthearted way.

Checking comprehension

Read the passage and then answer the questions below.

It's a mugger's game in Manhattan

(**Today we have a short story set in New York, the world's largest producer of adrenalin.**) Martin had lived in New York for 40 years and never been mugged once. This did not make him confident – on the contrary, it terrified him. The way he saw it, he was now the most likely person in Manhattan to get mugged next.

"What are the odds in favour of me getting mugged?" he asked his friend Lenny.

"How much are you willing to bet?" said Lenny, who was a compulsive gambler.

"Oh come on, this is too important to bet on!"

"Nothing is too important to bet on", said Lenny, shocked. That was the end of their friendship.

"How do you think I can avoid getting mugged?" Martin asked his friend Grace. Grace had not been outside her apartment in five years, as a sure-fire way of avoiding being mugged. It had failed; someone had broken in and mugged her.

"I've no idea, Martin", she said. "Most of these guys are on drugs anyway, and they need the money for their addiction."

This gave Martin an idea. If the muggers only needed the money for drugs, why didn't he offer them drugs instead? Then possibly they would be so grateful they wouldn't harm him. Through some rich friends he knew he bought small quantities of heroin, cocaine and LSD. He had never touched the stuff himself, so he had to label them carefully to make sure he didn't get them mixed up.

One day he was walking in a part of Central Park he shouldn't have been in (the part where there is grass and trees) when three men leapt out at him. One was black, one was Puerto Rican and one was Caucasian. Well, at least mugging is being integrated he thought.

"You want drugs?" he cried. "I've got drugs! Anything you want you can have. Just name it. But don't touch me!"

The three men let go of him respectfully.

"We almost made a big mistake there", said one of them. "This guy's a pusher. Hurt him, and we could have the Mafia down on us. Let's see what you got, mister."

Somewhat to his surprise Martin found himself displaying his wares to his clientele. Even more to his surprise, he found himself accepting money for the drugs, much more than he'd paid for them.

"How come you guys have all this money?" He said. "Why are you out mugging if you have money?"

"Well, we're not real muggers," said the Caucasian embarrassed. "We're out-of-

>>>→

work actors."

"I thought out-of-work show-biz people always became waiters or barmen", said Martin.

"Right. But there are so many showbiz people in catering now that you can't get work as waiters. So we had to get work as muggers."

When Martin got home, he bought some more drugs from his friend. Pretty soon he sold them to some more muggers. Pretty soon after that he found he was spending more and more time pushing drugs, and making more and more money at it. Being afraid of muggings had turned him into a professional drug-pusher.

One day a man leapt out at him and grabbed him.

"You want drugs?" said Martin. "I got drugs."

"I want money," said a familiar voice.

"Lenny!" cried Martin. "how're you doing?"

"Badly," said Lenny. "I lost everything gambling."

He hit Martin over the head and took his money, wallet and all his credit cards, leaving the little packets of white powder behind.

Moral: It's no use offering drugs to a money addict.

(Miles Kington in *The Times*)

a) Martin thought he was going to be mugged soon because:
   i)   everyone gets mugged at least once in forty years.
   ii) he had been mugged more than once before.
   iii) most people in New York get mugged sooner or later.

b) He decided to offer his muggers drugs because:
   i)   he had more drugs than money.
   ii) most muggers don't need the money.
   iii) most muggers are more interested in drugs than money.

c) When he was finally mugged, he wasn't harmed because:
   i)   the muggers thought he was protected by the Mafia.
   ii) the muggers were impressed by his readiness to co-operate with them.
   iii) he didn't have any money on him.

d) Martin assumed that most muggers:
   i)   didn't have much money.
   ii) were out-of-work actors.
   iii) worked in the catering business.

e) Martin was finally unable to save himself from being mugged properly because:
   i)   he was no longer Lenny's friend.
   ii) Lenny was also pushing drugs.
   iii) Lenny needed money and not drugs.

Writing summaries

1 Working in pairs, choose one of the passages. Write down the questions that a policeman would have asked the person who was mugged.

2 Form a new pair with a student who chose the same passage as you. Without looking back at the passages, ask or answer questions about what happened, and take notes.

3 Using your notes, write a short summary of one of the passages in no more than 150 words. When you have finished, re-read the relevant passage and make sure you have included all the necessary details.

Further work

1 Organise a class debate for and against the motion 'Mugging is a social problem rather than a serious crime'. Decide whether you are for or against the motion, and prepare a short speech expressing your opinions. If you wish, you can look in newspapers for further examples to support your argument.

2 Choose ten to fifteen words or expressions from these passages and write a paragraph describing what Martin will do to avoid being mugged in the future.

3 Look back over the passages in this unit and, if you have read them, the passages in units 40 and 41. Using as much of this new vocabulary as possible, write a paragraph or two on one of the following subjects.

   – Describe the legal system in your country.
   – 'Innocent until proved guilty? Or vice versa?' Describe the relationship between the police and the general public in your country.
   – Think of some new ways to deal with people who have committed less serious offences.

Unit 43 When a sense of nationhood goes off the rails. . .

This article is about racism and was written in 1984 by Roy Hattersley, a Member of Parliament and the Deputy Leader of the Labour Party.

Inferring

Read the passage and answer the questions below.

LAST WEEK, making a brief visit to the buffet car of a train which was fast approaching Coventry, a fellow passenger of-
5 fered me a sudden piece of un-solicited biographical informa-tion: 'I am not,' he said, 'a racist ...' leaving the sentence hang-ing in the early morning Mid-
10 land air as if I would take the 'but' for granted. He was right. Thanks to years of experience, I did.

It was an intrinsically strange
15 way for a complete stranger to begin a conversation. But it is not, in my experience, an un-usual form of introduction. Whenever I hear it employed I
20 reach for my conscience. For before the sentence is finished I can hear in my imagination the unmistakable sound of a cock crowing three times.
25 At the uncertain moment of first meeting an outstretched opinion I always feel that my well-mannered duty requires me to accept the assertions
30 that my brief acquaintances make about their conduct and character. I usually say, 'I'm sure you're not.' But the polite response invariably opens the way to a series of aggrieved
35 anecdotes which the complain-ant really believes to be wholly justified and which I regard as the product of flagrant, if un-conscious, prejudice.
40
As the tales of purple-painted front doors, arranged mar-riages, and ever-open grocery shops unfold, I know that I should react strongly. But I
45 simply mumble my dissent and edge my civilised way on to morally more certain ground.

My problem is that I feel sorry for the men and women
50 who really believe that they are justified in objecting to living next door to a mosque.

It is difficult to distinguish between invincible innocence
55 and indomitable ignorance. Most of the people who pro-claim their racial decency are consumed by the clichés of moral corruption. They honest-
60 ly think that what they say 'stands to reason' and is 'no more than common sense.'

They regularly tell me that they are expressing the opin-
65 ions of 'millions of men and women who are too frightened to speak out' because of 'the

200

activities of the race relations industry.' Some of them actually insist that 'in private you believe it too.' That is when pride drives out the civilised conventions.

Last week the particular variant of self-seductive nonsense to which I was subjected was a statement which my travelling irritant genuinely believed to be incontrovertible. 'If they live here,' he said, 'they ought to behave like us.' His objection was that Indians persisted in being Indian, that Muslims revered Mohammed and that Sikh bus conductors wear turbans instead of peak caps.

Yet when the circumstances of immigration were reversed, 'we' never even contemplated behaving like 'them'. The British in India never ever thought of assuming Indian ways. Indeed, a special term of abuse was invented for those deviants who did adopt the customs of the country in which they lived. They were said to have gone native – a description of their conduct which was more offensive to the host nation than it was to the occasional deviant visitor. I suppose that my travelling companion wanted the Asian British to go native. But he did not put his opinion in quite that language.

However, in one particular, the Indians have begun to copy our way of life. British visitors are now required to obtain entry certificates. I trust that they will not completely copy our habits. For I do not want to see English grannies locked up at Delhi airport, young Scotsmen refused brief holidays with their expatriate relations, and Welsh sisters accused of attempts to evade immigration regulations just because they forgot the name of the rugby club for which their brothers played back home. But no doubt it would gratify those people who want them to behave like us.

(Roy Hattersley in *The Guardian*)

The writer's choice of words and expressions tends to imply more than it states explicitly, probably because the passage deals with a rather delicate subject, and because the writer wants to draw attention to the irony implicit in many racist remarks. Look at the following extracts from the passage and answer the questions.

a) 'Thanks to years of experience, I did.' (lines 12–13)
   What do you infer from this sentence about the writer's reactions to the remark 'I am not a racist'?
b) 'But it is not, in my experience, an unusual form of introduction.' (lines 16–18)
   What does this imply about the writer's experience of racism?
c) 'As the tales of purple-painted front doors, arranged marriages, and ever-open grocery shops unfold. . .' (lines 41–4)
   Does this sentence refer to the habits and customs of the Asians or the British?
d) '. . .the activities of the race relations industry.' (lines 68–70)
   What do you think are the activities of the race relations industry?
e) 'His objection was that Indians persisted in being Indian. . .' (lines 82–7)
   Why is this an objection?

>>>→

f) 'They were said to have gone native. . .' (lines 98–9)
Why is this 'more offensive to the host nation than it was to the occasional deviant visitor'? (lines 100–3)

g) 'For I do not want to see English grannies locked up at Delhi airport, young Scotsmen refused brief holidays with their expatriate relations, and Welsh sisters accused of attempts to evade the immigration regulations just because they forgot the name of the rugby club for which their brothers played back home.' (lines 114–24)
   What does this imply about British immigration regulations? Does the writer think this acceptable or unacceptable treatment?

Understanding writer's style

The writer uses a number of rather flamboyant expressions. You may find that this feature of the style makes the passage more interesting; however, the meaning is sometimes obscured.

   What does the writer mean by the following phrases? Re-write them in a way that expresses their general sense more simply.

Example: 'But I simply mumble my dissent and edge my civilised way on to
            morally more certain ground.' (lines 45–8)
This could be rewritten:
   But I disagree and change the subject.

a) '. . .a fellow passenger offered me a sudden piece of unsolicited biographical information. . .' (lines 4–7)

b) 'At the uncertain moment of first meeting an outstretched opinion I always feel that my well-mannered duty requires me to accept the assertions that my brief acquaintances make about their conduct and character.' (lines 25–32)

c) 'But the polite response invariably opens the way to a series of aggrieved anecdotes which the complainant really believes to be wholly justified and which I regard as the product of flagrant, if unconscious, prejudice.' (lines 33–40)

d) 'That is when pride drives out the civilised conventions.' (lines 72–4)

e) 'Last week the particular variant of self-seductive nonsense to which I was subjected was a statement which my travelling irritant genuinely believed to be incontrovertible.' (lines 75–80)

f) 'His objection was that Indians persisted in being Indian, that Muslims revered Mohammed and that Sikh bus conductors wear turbans instead of peak caps.' (lines 82–7)

Writing summaries

1 This is a difficult passage to summarise because, although its subject is racism, it deals with three different points. These are:

- How the writer reacts to the comment 'I am not a racist' and why.
- How he reacts to 'In private you believe it too' and why.
- How he reacts to 'If they live here they ought to behave like us.'

Write notes on these three points.

2 Now write a short paragraph of no more than 120–150 words describing how the writer would react to the statement 'Immigrants should behave like the inhabitants of their adopted country'.

Reacting to the text

1 Work in pairs. How would you react to someone who began a conversation: 'I'm not a racist, but...' and then made a long list of racist statements like the man the writer met in the train?

2 How would you react if someone said 'Immigrants should behave like their hosts'?

Further work

1 Find out what percentage of the population of your country are immigrants. Prepare a short talk on the immigrants in your country, what they do and how they live. Do you think they are well-integrated into your country?

2 Form groups of three or four. Discuss whether anything can or should be done to stop immigration into your country or to deal with racism. Make a list of your suggestions. Then find out whether other groups in the class agree with your proposals. Organise a class discussion on the problems of immigration.

3 Choose ten to fifteen words or expressions from the passage. Use them in a paragraph or two which describes a personal experience of racism or an unpleasant attitude towards foreigners.

Unit 44   Lucy Rowan's mother

This passage is by Linda Blandford, a British journalist living in New York.

Extracting main ideas

Read the passage and answer the questions below.

Lucy Rowan's mother lives alone in Brooklyn. She has a one-roomed flat (rent: $125 a month) and her only income is her social security cheque for $196. Lucy's mother is 86; she has cataracts and arthritis. Until a few weeks ago she could still get about; she shopped, visited, went for walks. Her arthritis is so bad she can't move. Lucy would take her to live with her family but daughter Lisa would have to   5
sleep on the sofa. Is that a fair long-term solution? Sister Bernice talked briefly of moving her into a nursing home. The fact that only 3 per cent of the city's elderly live in institutions tells all about its nursing homes.

So that was the situation last month. One day, on the way home, Lucy noticed a dramatic poster in the bus. It showed a mail box stuffed with letters. 'The lady in   10
3B is dying,' ran the headline, 'only her mailbox can save her.' There was a telephone number for something called Early Alert run by the city's Department for the Ageing.

Not expecting too much (making contact with officialdom often seems as easy as making contact with outer space), Lucy telephoned the number. Early Alert is a   15
project specializing in stuffed mail boxes. However, a patient and understanding official gave Lucy a whole string of phone numbers to try and much encouraging information.

Lucy's mother, it seems, has not been getting all the benefits she is entitled to. Ninety-one per cent of New York's elderly base their income, as she does, on   20
social security. Getting even that isn't easy.

Anyone retiring now who has worked consistently for the last forty quarters and has paid exactly the right contributions is entitled to a minimum of $107.90 a month. Since that's patently not enough to live on, there's Supplementary Security Income. Combining the two: a single person receives $248.65 a month unless he or   25
she isn't entitled to social security, in which case, and for no discernible reason, the SSI income is only $228.65. The official poverty level in New York is $250 a month.

Of course there's Medicaid providing all manner of home help and paying medical bills. And food stamps and even welfare from the city, if there still isn't enough. Being entitled to all this is not the same as finding out how to get it. As the   30
official put it: 'The trouble is that no one knows how the whole thing works.' Still Lucy felt encouraged that she could work her way through the red tape.

She rang the Brooklyn office of the Department for the Ageing. Indeed her mother should be getting more money, visitors to help her with 'household chores, money management, personal care, laundry, meal-planning, nutrition, shopping, seeing a doctor'. 35

Unfortunately she would have to be seen by a welfare worker to make an inventory of her health and worldly goods. Someone should be able to come and see her in a few weeks. But what about now? This was an emergency, Lucy explained. The official offered the telephone number of a private employment agency: household helps, $7 an hour, six hours daily minimum. 40

Lucy moved her mother into her apartment the next morning: daughter Lisa took to the sofa.

Despite cut-backs, the city does everything it can think of to help the old. It sets up centres and projects. Most of them disappear before people can find them. 45 Others complain they can't find the shut in, isolated old to help. But every time bureaucracy comes up with another way to tackle one problem, it runs into yet another problem.

Early Alert is the perfect example. It's available to anyone over 65. This is the theory: nearly all the city's mail is delivered to boxes clustered together on the 50 ground floor of each building (except for those that don't have boxes). Through a tie in with post offices, Early Alert arranges for the postman to put a red dot inside the relevant box to remind himself it belongs to an old person. If he notices a bulging wad of letters, the postman remembers and works out that something might be amiss. 55

Not surprisingly, only 11,000 people have registered so far with Early Alert. Most old people are afraid to. Breaking open mail boxes is so common that people don't want to alert criminals to their vulnerability. Besides not many old people get letters.

Undaunted, the Department for the Ageing came up with a brand new scheme. They opened a pilot Senior Citizens' Crime Prevention and Assistance Centre. 60 Bearing in mind that 40 per cent of the inner city's elderly poor have been the victims of crime, the centre wanted to teach the other 60 per cent to protect themselves. It offered booklets with such tips as 'If awakened at night by an intruder, lie still'.

It would also help people after they have been mugged. Social workers will offer 65 counselling to help post-mugging trauma and, on a more practical level, make the necessary telephone calls to get stolen ID cards replaced and to find emergency financial and housing help if necessary.

The problem? The office is on the sixth floor of an unguarded, almost deserted building in a rough street off Broadway. There is no elevator attendant. The 70 Crime Prevention Centre always advises the elderly not to get into empty elevators.

Lucy Rowan discovered that to get help for her mother, she had to contact seven different agencies. Her mother has since died.

(Linda Blandford: *America on Five Valium a Day*)

1 With your partner, write down the sequence of events described in the passage, from the moment Lucy Rowan's mother needed help to when the old lady died.
2 Now write down everything that the city authorities do or have done to help old people. Then make notes on why these efforts are not very successful.
3 Write a one or two line summary of the passage's main ideas.

Inferring

Partly because of the writer's style and partly because the passage is an extract from a longer text, a certain amount of information is implied rather than directly stated explicitly. Look at the following sentences and answer the questions.

a) 'Sister Bernice talked briefly of moving her into a nursing home.' (lines 6–7)
   Who do you think Sister Bernice is?
b) 'The fact that only 3 per cent of the city's elderly live in institutions tells all about its nursing homes.' (lines 7–8)
   So what does this fact suggest?
c) 'The lady in 3B is dying.' (lines 10–11)
   What do you think 3B refers to?
d) 'If he notices a bulging wad of letters, the postman remembers and works out that something might be amiss.' (lines 53–5)
   Why would he work out that something might be wrong?
e) 'Breaking open mail boxes is so common that people don't want to alert criminals to their vulnerability.' (lines 57–8)
   Why would this alert criminals to their vulnerability?
f) 'The Crime Prevention Centre always advises the elderly not to get into empty elevators.' (lines 70–1)
   Why do they advise this?

Understanding writer's style

There are several interesting features of the writer's style in this passage. One feature is the absence of discourse markers to signal the relationship between two sentences or paragraphs. To make sense of the sentences, the reader has to infer this relationship.
For example: 'Until a few weeks ago she could still get about. . .'
             'Her arthritis is so bad now she can't move.'
In the context, the discourse marker *but* could begin the second sentence, in order to stress the contrast with the first. The effect of this style is to suggest a sense of inevitability about the sequence of events.

Look at the following sentences and decide what the relationship is between the sentence pairs, and what discourse marker could be inserted to make this relationship explicit. There may be more than one possibility in certain cases.

a) 'Ninety-one per cent of New York's elderly base their income, as she does, on social security. Getting even that isn't easy.' (lines 20–1)
b) 'This was an emergency, Lucy explained. The official offered the telephone number of a private employment agency. . .' (lines 39–41)

c) 'Lucy moved her mother into her apartment the next morning: daughter Lisa took to the sofa.' (lines 42–3)
d) 'Most old people are afraid to. Breaking open mail boxes is so common that people don't want to alert criminals to their vulnerability.' (lines 56–8)
e) 'Lucy Rowan discovered that to get help for her mother, she had to contact seven different agencies. Her mother has since died.' (lines 72–3)

Further work

1 Work in groups of three or four. Do similar problems with old people occur in your country or countries? If so, can anything be done to help? If not, why not? Who do you think should be responsible for the welfare of old people? The State or their families?

2 Working in groups of three or four, make a list of all the problems facing old people who live alone. Then think of ways in which the following people or services might be able to help:

- social services   – transport authorities
- neighbours   – family
- police   – door-to-door delivery services
- postal services

Write a letter with your suggestions to a local paper.

3 Choose ten to fifteen words or expressions from the passage and write the dialogue that Lucy had with the 'patient and understanding official' in line 00 onwards.

Unit 45 Looking on the bright side

The following passage was written by Bernard Levin, an English journalist who is well-known for his rather complex style.

Checking comprehension

Read the passage and answer the questions below.

IT IS WELL known that no news is good news; what is less widely understood is that good news is bad news. And this particular bit of truly significant news has not yet, apparently, penetrated to China, where the authorities have decreed, according to a report by the *Daily Telegraph*'s 5 inquisitive and entertaining Peking correspondent, Graham Earnshaw, that only good news is to be reported, and that stories of such negative matters as crime and corruption are no longer to be published.

It won't work I'm afraid. The heirs of Mao are only the 10 latest in the long line of those who have dreamed the same dream; that if you do not draw attention to the darkness, it will turn to light of its own accord. The hunger is constantly making itself felt in this country, too; it's a poor month that doesn't see a letter in one newspaper or another complain- 15 ing that the press prints only bad news. Yet a newspaper which published nothing but that which can be seen through rose-coloured spectacles would speedily find its readers deserting in their numbers to rivals unafraid of pointing out that life is not altogether a bowl of cherries, 20 and the only reason that such a fate will not overtake the Chinese papers under the new dispensation is that readers have no rival sheets to desert to.

The problem can be summed up in a dozen words: we do not wish to be told that which we already know. We 25 know that most husbands do not murder their wives, that

208

few bank managers abscond with the funds, that although
some aeroplanes crash, far more arrive safely, that not
every dog will bite. And we know these things for a reason
far deeper and more important than that provided by the   30
statistics which bear out our convictions. We are instinc-
tively possessed of the truth that the universe runs on the
principle that the bad is the exception to the good.

And it follows from this that what attracts our attention
and awakens our interest is the exception, which means,   35
broadly speaking, the bad news. A headline reading
'Nearly 55,000,000 people not struck by lightning in
Britain last year' will not sell newspapers, nor will it
deserve to. And I cannot believe that things are any
different in China, where a news item in the *People's Daily*   40
recording the fact that practically all the wheat sown the
previous spring had grown upwards rather than down-
wards is unlikely to have the readers spilling their breakfast coffee into their laps in their excitement.

Crime in China will not diminish merely because the   45
newspapers are forbidden to mention it, nor will the
incidence of corruption among Chinese officials or politicians be less because there is a general pretence that
there isn't any. In Paradise, no doubt, nothing unpleasant
ever happens. Here below, other standards obtain. When   50
mosques or synagogues are built, a patch or a corner of the
building is always left unfinished; perfection belongs only
to Allah or Jehovah, and it is not for men to pretend to it.
In China, however, though they do not believe they are
already perfect, they believe that by telling each other that   55
they are they will presently come to be.

(Bernard Levin: *Speaking Up*)

Decide whether the following statements are true or false according to the passage.

a) The Chinese authorities do not think that good news is bad news.
b) In the future, bad news will no longer be reported in China.
c) According to the writer, it is only the Chinese who think that bad news should not be reported.
d) Newspapers would soon lose their readers if they only reported good news.
e) Statistics prove that there is more bad news than good.
f) Readers are more interested in the unexceptional.
g) In China as elsewhere, people are likely to be interested in the exceptional.
h) Suppressing bad news will help reduce crime and corruption.
i) According to the writer, man should not forget that he is imperfect.

Understanding writer's style

1 The writer uses a number of expressions which are fairly literary and not often
   used in everyday speech. As a result you may find them difficult to understand.
   Look at the following sentences and the clues to their meaning.
   Re-write them more simply.

   a) '...if you do not draw attention to the darkness, it will turn to light of its own
      accord.' (lines 12–13)
      The images 'darkness' and 'light' both refer to something already mentioned
      in the first paragraph. What? What do these people think will happen to this
      darkness if it is ignored?
   b) 'Yet a newspaper which published nothing but that which can be seen
      through rose-coloured spectacles would speedily find its readers deserting in
      their numbers to rivals...' (lines 16–19)
      Is 'rose-coloured' a pleasant or unpleasant colour? How would you see the
      world if you looked at it through 'rose-coloured spectacles'? How would you
      see it when you took them off? So what is the effect of these spectacles? And
      what kind of news would you see?
   c) '...life is not altogether a bowl of cherries...' (line 20)
      Does the whole phrase suggest that life is pleasant or unpleasant?
   d) '...to have the readers spilling their breakfast coffee into their laps in their
      excitement.' (lines 43–4)
      Would news of wheat growing upwards be exciting or not?

2 The writer uses irony on several occasions in which he says one thing but means
   exactly the opposite. Can you find these examples of irony in the passage?

Extracting main ideas

1 Read the passage again and note down the line numbers of the sentences which
   contain what you consider to be the main ideas of the passage.

2 Check your answers with another student. Do you both agree?

3 The passage makes two main points: the first one might be described as the
   superficial reason for writing the passage; the second is a more philosophical
   reflection which is generated by the first. Look at the statements below and
   decide which one best summarises the first point, and which one expresses most
   accurately the second.

   a) Newspapers have a responsibility for reporting bad as well as good news.
   b) Man is imperfect and it is no use hoping that words will change this.
   c) Truth cannot be filtered and controlled by the Press.

d) Newspapers wish to report the news while governments wish to suppress it.
e) Instinct tells us that there is no good news without bad news.
f) It is only exceptional news which interests people, and exceptional news is usually bad.

Writing summaries

Write a summary of the passage in about 120–150 words. Don't forget to re-read the passage when you have finished, and to check that you have included all the main ideas.

Further work

1 Work in groups of three or four. Take a newspaper and choose one or two articles which contain bad news. Try and re-write them in a more optimistic way. When everyone has finished, collect all the articles which the others in your class have written and make a 'Good News' class magazine.

2 Look back over the passage in this unit and, if you have read them, the passages in units 43 and 44. Note down twenty or so words and expressions which you have learnt. Then, using as much of this new vocabulary as possible, write a paragraph or two on one of the following subjects:

– Should the news ever be censored?
– Describe a meeting on a train with a stranger who turns out to disagree with everything you believe in. Write the conversation you have.
– Describe a day in your life when you are old.

Acknowledgements

The authors and publishers are grateful to the following for permission to reproduce copyright material:

p.6, Patricia Marne and *Company* magazine; p.10, From *An Innocent Millionaire* by Stephen Vizinczey, published in the United Kingdom by Hamish Hamilton Ltd and in the United States by Atlantic Monthly Press; p.14, p.32, p.168, p.36, p.44, London Express News and Feature Services; p.19, From *Mondays Thursdays* by Keith Waterhouse published by Michael Joseph; p.23, From *Down and Out in Paris and London*, copyright 1933 by George Orwell, renewed 1961 by Sonia Pitt-Rivers, reprinted by permission of Harcourt Brace Jovanovich, Inc. and the estate of the late Sonia Brownell Orwell and Secker and Warburg Ltd; p.27, Associated Newspapers Group plc; p.39, Metropolitan Police; p.40, The National Trust; p.48, Sterling Lord Agency, Inc.; p.52, Reproduced by permission of *Punch*; p.56, p.76, Reprinted by permission of *American Way*, inflight magazine of American Airlines, copyright 1983 by American Airlines; p.60, p.72, p.92, p.130, p.141, p.150, p.172, p.188, Reproduced by courtesy of *The Observer*, London*; p.65, Matthew Clark and Sons Ltd for the advertisement for Jameson's Irish whiskey; p.67, Crest Hotels International; p.68, Collett, Dickenson, Pearce and Partners Ltd Advertising, for the advertisement for the Army; p.80 (8.1.84), p.97 (Autumn 1983), p.180 (24.7.83), p.130 (17.6.84), p.162 (2.5.82), Times Newspapers Ltd; p.84, Copyright Gerald Durrell, reproduced by permission of Curtis Brown Ltd, London, from *Three Singles to Adventure*, Granada Publishing Ltd; p.88, World Wildlife Fund; p.101, From *The Book of Ages* by Desmond Morris, copyright © 1983 by Desmond Morris, reprinted by permission of Viking Penguin Inc. and Jonathan Cape Ltd; p.104, Reproduced by kind permission of the Health Education Council, London; p.108, Victor Keegan; p.114, Reprinted from the May 10th, 1983 issue of *Family Circle Magazine*, © 1985 The Family Circle Inc.; p.120, From *One's Company*, the estate of Peter Fleming and Jonathan Cape Ltd; p.124, Royal Academy of Arts, Arts Council, National Portrait Gallery, for their pamphlets; p.130, *Ms London*; p.136, Gillon Aitken; p.144, 147, Syndication International Ltd; p.155, Multimedia Publications; p.158, Victor Zorza; p.176, From *Philip Garner's Better Living Catalogue*, Sidgwick and Jackson Ltd and Delilah Books; p.182, *Radio Times*; p.194, Giles Gordon; p.197, Miles Kington; p.200, The Rt Hon. Roy Hattersley MP; p.204, From *America on Five Valium a*

---

* *The Observer* publishes a resource pack of authentic source materials for teachers of EFL. In nine monthly packs, from October to June, over 150 *Observer* articles are used, each with a specially written worksheet and exercises. Available by subscription only, further details from: *The Observer* EFL Service, 8 St Andrew's Hill, London EC4V 5JA.

Day by Linda Blandford, Methuen London and Hughes Massie; p.208, From *Speaking Up*, copyright © Bernard Levin 1982, reproduced by permission of Curtis Brown Ltd, London and Jonathan Cape Ltd.

Photographs on pp.166–7, King's College Chapel, Cambridge: Royal Commission on Historical Monuments, Crown Copyright; Laura Ashley dress, ashtray by Nigel Luckhurst: Cambridge University Press; The Parthenon, Athens: The Mansell Collection; chair by John Honey: The Design Council; *The Hay Wain* by John Constable, reproduced by courtesy of the Trustees, The National Gallery, London; toaster, watch by Gered Mankowitz: London Express News and Feature Services.

Artwork by Wenham Arts and Geoff Green
Book design by Peter Ducker MSTD